Dear Fellow Warrior,

**By
Sharisse Scott-Rawlins**

Copyright

Copyright © 2025 by Sharisse Scott-Rawlins
All rights reserved.

No part of this publication may be reproduced, distributed, or transmitted in any form or by any means—electronic, mechanical, photocopying, recording, or otherwise—without the prior written permission of the copyright owner, except in the case of brief quotations used in critical reviews, articles, or academic references.

This is a work of original nonfiction and poetry.

All writing, design, and layout are the sole property of the author: interior design, and all written content by Sharisse Scott-Rawlins. Book Cover Design by 4N House Designs. Author Photo by Shots by Rambo.

Typeset in Times New Roman, 11 pt.
Trim size: 5.5" x 8.5"
Printed and published independently via Kindle Direct Publishing. **First Edition, 2025**
ISBN: [979-8-9995521-8-1]

For rights requests, speaking engagements, or collaborations, contact Sharisse Scott-Rawlins directly.
Email: **DEARFELLOWWARRIOR@GMAIL.COM** |
Social Media: **@DEARFELLOWWARRIOR**

Dedication

To my *Fellow Warriors,* —
The ones who know what it means to fight in silence,
to rise without applause,
to carry hope like a hidden flame.

This book is for you.
The Warrior Society—
survivors, fighters, healers, and truth-tellers
who remind the world that resilience has a heartbeat,
and strength has many names.

Thank you to the arms that held me
when I couldn't hold myself.
To the legs that moved me
when my will was too weary.
To the body that became my battleground
and still chose to bloom.

That Warrior spirit carried me through the most difficult time of my life. And together, we made it through the fire.

That spirit lives in you, *too.*

(Write your name here and claim your healing.)

Preface

I was twenty-two years old, sitting through eight-hour chemotherapy infusions in a hospital room that had no idea what to do with my big dreams, when the idea for this book first came to me.

A tumor had been growing silently inside my throat since I was twenty-one—slowly stealing my voice, silencing the girl I was, and awakening the woman I was destined to become.

The words started as whispers—quiet reflections scribbled between appointments, prayers in the form of poems. What began as a means of survival slowly transformed into something more sacred:
A story.
A voice.
A return to self.

I finished this book in the place I consider my sanctuary: Martha's Vineyard. On the sacred shores of Inkwell Beach—where I've been writing poetry since I was eleven—I found my rhythm again. At the meeting point of ink and ocean, I remembered who I was.

Dear Fellow Warrior, came to life over eight years on those healing shores, where the tides mirror thought and beauty lives in the space between words. There, by the water's edge, I learned to embrace the ebb and flow of ideas—to listen to the ocean's pulse, which echoed the quiet, persistent rhythm within me.

The shore taught me that words, like waves, are ever-shifting yet constant. That poetry isn't just language—it's presence. That the deepest truths often live in silence, in the pause, in the space between the lines.

This collection traces reflection, growth, and becoming. Each poem is a wave. Each line, a tide. Together, they carry the lessons I've learned in surrender, resilience, presence, and truth.

May these words carry you inward, as the tides once held me. May you find your own safe space along the shore.

When I started this journey, I was surviving.
I was hiding.
I was searching for myself.

And in many ways, I was writing this book to find *her*.

There are so many versions of me in these pages—
The girl who loved words but didn't always love herself.
The girl who covered her insecurities with achievements.
The girl who knew how to show up for everyone else, but rarely for herself. The version of me who quietly believed that if she just created something beautiful enough, maybe people would finally see her.
Maybe, she would finally see herself.

What I didn't realize was that I wouldn't understand the power of my voice until I became voiceless.

The first sign I needed to speak up came when I was fighting cancer in silence—when doctors dismissed my pain, and no one listened, until the tumor had grown so large I physically couldn't speak.

By the time they heard me, I had already been silenced.

That moment changed everything.
It taught me that using your voice is not a luxury—it's a responsibility.

From a creative standpoint, I always knew I had a gift. Even when I doubted everything else, I never doubted that. I knew I was chosen. Destined. Called.

But purpose doesn't always arrive with clarity.
Sometimes, it comes wrapped in chaos.

I had to walk through trials, tribulations, and long seasons of silence to get here.
But I made it.
I'm still here.
And I'm still becoming.

I launched my brand *bySharisse* in 2010, at just fifteen years old—sketching designs between classes and turning my bedroom into a mini studio.

Back then, it was about creating one-of-a-kind pieces that helped me express the parts of myself (and my clients) we didn't yet have words for. But over time, it became something greater.

Today, *bySharisse* is more than a fashion brand.
It's a pledge.
A living, breathing safe space—stitched from my story, shaped by my spirit, and built to welcome others in.

It is a vessel for protection, upliftment, and creative truth-telling.
A reminder that you don't have to do it all alone.

I didn't know, at twenty-two, that this book would take me years to finish. I didn't know I would live through even more love, loss, and transformation than I ever imagined. I didn't know that the girl who started writing in the waiting room would become a woman who survived—not just cancer, but burnout. Betrayal. Grief. Life.

The invisible weight of being Black, brilliant, and brave in a world that often doesn't know what to do with any of that.

But here I am.
Here we are.
And this book is part of that journey.

But this is more than a poetry book.

It's a safe space.
A conversation.

A mirror.
A survival story written in real time.

A space for the younger me, the present me, and the woman I'm still becoming.

A space for you— If you've ever searched for yourself in your own reflection. If you've ever needed a place to be soft and strong at the same time. If you've ever wanted to feel seen—not for the roles you play, but for the soul you carry.

Inside these pages, you'll find letters to the self—past, present, and future.
Words that remember what it felt like to fall apart.
Words that dare to believe healing is still possible.

Each poem begins with an open letter—a message to the Warrior within.
Each ends with a reflection prompt—an invitation to go deeper, to turn the gaze inward, and to write your own way through.

This is for the Warriors who learned to shine while carrying shadows. For the Warriors still learning to rest without guilt. For anyone who's ever had to reintroduce themselves to themselves.

You don't need to be a poet to feel at home here.
You just need a heartbeat, a little courage, and the willingness to be seen.

Let these words hold you.
Challenge you.
Heal you.

Let them remind you that your story matters.
And that you were never alone in the fight.

Welcome to ***Dear Fellow Warrior,***

Table of Contents

I. The Awakening
The Egg — The Moment of Origin
When everything you knew becomes what you must fight to keep.

II. The Crawl Toward Clarity
The Caterpillar — Stillness, Grief, and Growing Pains
When becoming means undoing who you thought you had to be.

III. The Quiet Metamorphosis
The Chrysalis — Confined but Transforming
Where healing happens in silence, and transformation takes root unseen.

IV. The Emergence
The Wings Unfold — When the Light Gets In
Where the becoming begins — bold, soft, and true.

V. The Ascension
The Wings — Reborn in Truth, Carried by Grace
You've earned your wings. Now, you rise.

I. The Awakening

The Egg — The Moment of Origin
When everything you knew becomes what you must fight to keep

This is the moment everything shifts.
Before the wings, before the flight—there is a rupture.
A diagnosis. A loss. A betrayal.
Something that cracks you open without warning.

You didn't ask to be broken.
But you were.
Like an egg on the edge of a leaf,
resting in the quiet before the chaos—
You were placed gently in the world,
then shaken.

Sometimes it's an illness.
Sometimes it's heartbreak,
a silence too loud,
a blow that splits your peace in two.
They gave it a name.
But you gave it a fight.

This is where the battle begins—
not with fists, but with breath.
With fear pulsing behind your ribs.
With faith you weren't sure you still had.
With the trembling decision to keep going
when everything says to stop.

The Awakening is never gentle.
But it is sacred.
Because this is the moment
you begin again—
not by choice, but by necessity.

For me, it was cancer.
For you, it may be something else.
But the weight of the world changed for us both.

Here is where I begin.
Here is where *we* begin—
cracked, shaken,
but not broken.

Safe Space

for the Warrior learning that home begins within

Dear Fellow Warrior,
Some lessons arrive like whispers, others like thunder.
This is your warning bell.
Let this poem stir you.
Shake you.
Remind you: You don't want to wait until a crisis hits to go searching for peace.
You are worthy of safety now.
Create it. Name it. Protect it.
Before the storm.

Breath—short.
Steps—quick.
The air behind me breaks
like glass shattering in slow motion.

Something's coming.
I don't know what—
but I know it wants pieces of me.

Streetlights blink
like warning signs.
Alley shadows whisper my name.
I duck. I run.
I search for locks, doors,
windows that promise:
"You're safe here."

But every place echoes back:
not enough, not safe, not yet.

My chest is thunder.
My legs— liars made of lead.

Walls close in.
Corners vanish.
Every turn becomes a question mark
that curves like fear.

I'm running fast,
but time runs faster.
Heart's a drum— disaster plastered
on the walls of mind and bone.
I swear I'm out here all alone.

Shadows stretch
like crooked hands,
grabbing at my life's demands.
Sirens blare inside my head—
I'm not sure if I've fled or bled.

Every echo sounds like threat,
a promise soaked in cold regret.
Every step— a warning sign:
They're coming,
and this breath
ain't mine.

I look for doors that never close,
a place where panic never grows.

A light, a lock, a hiding place—
a prayer, a whisper, wrapped in grace.

But walls won't hold what's built on fear,
and every mirror draws me near.

I search outside with trembling limbs,
not knowing safety starts within.

And then— stillness.
The kind that isn't outside.
It's in me.

The dark doesn't chase me anymore.
Because I stopped running.

I closed my eyes,
not to hide,
but to listen.

And I heard it—
the slow, steady knock
of my own heartbeat saying:
You're already here.

The safe space
isn't some hidden room.
It's not under floorboards,
not behind fences or fire escapes.
It's me.
It's always been me.

No one enters
unless I say so.
No storm breaks through
unless I open the window.
No voice grows louder than mine
unless I lower the volume of self.

They knock— but I don't have to let them in.
They shout— but I define my skin.
They push— but I am not the wall.
They pull— but I don't have to fall.

I am the silence they can't shatter.
I am the door they can't break.

The safe space isn't made of stone.
It's not a house, it's not a phone.
It's breath, it's truth,
it's inner ground—
where I remain when fear surrounds.

I am the place the storm can't shake.
The line no lie is strong enough to break.
The calm no chaos can erase—
I am, forever, my safe space.

~

Reflection Prompt: *Coming Home to You*

- Where do you find your safe space within yourself?

- What does that inner sanctuary feel like, sound like, look like?
- How can you protect and nurture that space today, especially when the world feels overwhelming?
- What boundary, ritual, or reminder helps you return to your inner calm when fear tries to pull you away?

Cancer Has Taken Over Me

for the Warrior who faced the unthinkable and found her voice anyway

---

Dear Fellow Warrior,
There are days when it feels like your body betrays you,
when your voice trembles beneath the weight of what
you've endured.
This poem was born in that place—
where fear sits in your throat,
and grief disguises itself as survival.
You are not alone in that moment.
This piece holds your hand there.

Inhale—
now take a deep breath out.
Five massive fingers grip my neck,
each fingerprint carving wounds

into the crevices of my throat.
I can't breathe.

The pressure scorches through my skin.
I try to scream for help—
but her thumb crushes my windpipe.
I'm suffocating.

My hands clutch at nothing—
grasping for light, for air,
for a name that doesn't belong to this body anymore.

I fight with all my might—
but nothing pries this oppressor loose.

My body goes numb—
crushed by catastrophe,
folded in on itself.
I feel nothing but defeat.
I'm turning blue—

My mind races,
a storm of static and disbelief:
What did I do to deserve this call?

Lymphoma.
The name lands like a verdict.
Lymphoma—
the fiercest oppressor I've known.

She is relentless.
Wrapped around my throat like a noose,
dragging me inside her shadowed grip,

offering no chance to stand—
only silence.

I scream—
but no one hears.
She clamps down on my voice,
muffling every plea,
clouding every thought.

This can't be happening—
Not to me.

But it is.

When her grip loosens,
just enough for one breath, one whisper—
I speak.

My name is Sharisse.
Cancer has taken over me.

But the truth—
my truth—
will set me free.

This is my story.
Not hers.
This is my self-discovery.
And it begins
with breath.

~

Reflection Prompt: *Reclaiming the Story*

- What does it mean to reclaim your story from something that feels overwhelming?
- What moments in your life have silenced you—and what would it look like to speak through them?
- How can your truth become a source of freedom, rather than fear?
- What part of your story still needs to be said aloud—even if your voice shakes?

The Risk to Be Alive

dedicated to the voice within me— the one that whispered, then screamed, then roared— even when no one listened. You saved my life.

Dear Fellow Warrior,
To live fully is to risk deeply—
love, loss, failure, and the unknown.
This poem is an ode to the bravery it takes
to show up anyway,
cracked open
and still choosing life.

With only the clothes on my back
and a 53% charged phone,

we moved—
my mother and I—
bodies in motion,
faith doing all the heavy lifting.

The elevator hummed
to the 11th floor:
CANCER CENTER
in bold white letters,
welcoming me into the unknown.

Check-in.
Undress.
Hospital gown.
They were expecting me.

Each room a mirror of misery.
Grief floated in sterile air,
and soon it brushed right through my hair.

I wish I could tell you it wasn't that bad—
but it was.

All those months
they said I was crying wolf
while a 12mm tumor
grew from my throat
to my lungs,
pressing against my heart.

And during those same months,
I was completing the hardest year of college—
my senior year.

Balancing master's-level coursework,
holding onto my GPA,
overworking myself into silence,
all while sensing something was deeply wrong.
Still, I showed up.
Still, I finished.
Still, I graduated at the top of my class.
Because resilience doesn't always look like healing.
Sometimes, it looks like survival with your head held high.

We caught it *"just in time,"*
but I still ask:
What if they had listened?
What if I had yelled louder?
What if I hadn't accepted
"It's just stress"?

I know now:
Trust your instincts.
You know your body
better than they ever will.

But still, the mind wanders
down *"what if"* roads
with no clear destination.

We punish ourselves
for what we couldn't predict.

Let me tell you something:
You did not deserve this.

You did nothing wrong.
This is not your fault.

I needed reasons—
but the reason never came.
No family history.
No smoking.
No warnings.

Even the doctors called it a mystery.

So I learned:
Life is not a puzzle to solve,
but a fire to feel.

And so I live now
like it matters—
because it does.

I don't know what tomorrow holds,
but today, I will hold myself.
Tightly. Boldly.

Aggressive Non-Hodgkin's Lymphoma.
The name alone feels like war.

My immune system under siege,
my youth now a liability in the eyes of medicine.

Too young for this.
Too rare for them.

But I— I am ready.

They say chemo may leave scars
that will continue to show up years from now…
And that I may survive this fight
only to face another.

But hear me clearly:
I will not remove my crown.
Not for confusion.
Not for pity.
Not for statistics.

I was built for this battle.
My body may tremble,
but my spirit—
my spirit is titanium.

So play it loud:
"Warrior Healer" by Geminelle on repeat.

Because I am
both the wounded and the one doing the healing.

And this—
this is the risk we take to be fully,
wildly, unapologetically alive.

~

Reflection Prompt: *The Bold Choice to Live*

- What risks have you taken to claim your life and your voice?

- When have you chosen yourself even when it terrified you?
- How do you hold your crown steady through the storms that try to shake it?
- What scars—physical or emotional—have shaped your fire, not dimmed it?
- What would it mean to live boldly and unapologetically right now?

You Should Have Listened

for every woman who knew something was wrong—and was told to wait

---

Dear Fellow Warrior,
Some pain doesn't come with a scream—it comes in whispers we were taught to ignore.
This poem lives in that moment.
The space between knowing something is wrong and being told, over and over, that you're fine.
It's about the unbearable weight of being unheard, especially as a Black woman the world expects to be strong, silent, and always "okay."
But we are allowed to break.
We are allowed to be believed.
And we must learn to believe ourselves—
the first time.

There's a point where tired
turns into terror.
But nobody tells you
when that line is crossed.

It starts small.
A tickle in your throat.
A headache that overstays.
A tightness that whispers,
"Pay attention."

But you don't.
You push through.
Because you're used to feeling off
and being told you're fine.

Midterms.
Back-to-back meetings.
A calendar colored in stress.
I was keeping pace with pressure
like it was a paycheck.
No time to slow down.
No room to fall apart.

I told myself I was just tired.
Just rundown.
Just being dramatic.
Because that's what they've always told us, right?
Black girls are dramatic.
Strong.
Resilient.

Overreacting.
Made of something tougher.

So I swallowed the ache.
I wore concealer over the shadows under my eyes
and pride over the panic in my chest.
I waited it out.

Until waiting felt like drowning.

I walked to the nurse's office
like my body was leading the way
without me.
I don't remember the walk.
Just the weight.
The knowing.
Something wasn't right.

Still, I sat in that waiting room—
surrounded by sniffles and sore throats—
telling myself I didn't belong there.
That I wasn't sick enough.
That someone else deserved the care more than me.
Even then,
I didn't fully listen
to me.

They told me to rest.
Take fluids.
Come back if it gets worse.
It did.
It got worse fast.

A scream behind my eyes.
A fire in my throat.
The kind of pain
that makes you forget how to be polite.

And I came back.
Again.
And again.
And again.

Five visits to different doctors before someone took me seriously.
Before a scan.
Before the words that changed everything.

And suddenly,
every moment I didn't trust myself
felt like betrayal.
I had begged with my body.
Whispered with symptoms.
Cried with silence.
But no one heard me.
Not even me.

They said it wasn't that serious.
But it was.
They said I looked fine.
But I wasn't.

They told me I was strong—
as if strength was the same as wellness,
as if Black girls can't fall apart.

Let me tell you something:
Being strong doesn't mean being silent.
Being strong doesn't mean being ignored.
Being strong doesn't mean being left to rot
in the waiting room of your own life.

I want to scream.
But even now— even now—
I know the world prefers me quiet.

So this is not a scream.
This is a siren. A flare.

To every woman who said something felt wrong
and was told she was fine.
To every girl who second-guessed her gut
because the system gaslit her symptoms.
To every Warrior
wearing a smile while her body unraveled—
You are not crazy.
You are not dramatic.
You are not too much.
You are right.

They should have listened.
And next time,
so will you.

~

Reflection Prompt: *Listen Before It's Loud*

- What early warning signs—physical, emotional, or spiritual—have you ignored before being forced to pay attention?
- How has the world's perception of your strength made it harder for you to seek or receive care?
- What would it look like to trust your inner knowing the first time it whispers, *"Something's not right"*?
- Who are the people in your life who truly listen when you speak—and how can you become that listener for yourself?
- What support systems do you need to advocate for your health, your rest, your voice?
- How can you begin honoring your well-being now, before the alarms become impossible to ignore?

Fifteen and Full-Time

for the girl who made magic before she knew what it would cost

---

Dear Fellow Warrior,
When your gift shows up early, so does the pressure. This one's for the ones who were told they were "special" before they were old enough to know what that

really meant.
For the ones who were praised for their potential,
but rarely asked if they were okay.
If perfection ever became your prison,
if your success ever silenced your struggle—
this poem is yours.

I made the Dean's List
every semester.
Graduated top of my class.
Trophies lined up like proof
that I deserved the love
I kept trying to earn.

But I only remember the D.
The one math test that wrecked me.
The shame. The spiral.
The punishment I gave myself
was harsher than anything
my parents could've imagined.

Even they said—
"Please... be easier on yourself."
But how could I?
I was the gifted one.
The girl with the brand.
The girl with the plan.
The girl who didn't have time
to fall apart.

By fifteen,
I wasn't just a fashion designer—

I was a full-time entrepreneur.
Before I even had a learner's permit,
I was learning how to market,
manage,
and master an industry
that never stopped spinning.

They told me it was impressive.
I thought it was survival.

My business was my first child,
my first love,
my first heartbreak,
my only mirror.
I poured everything into it.
And somewhere along the way,
I forgot how to just be.

I was sewing in between classes,
sketching between sprints,
building a brand
while my body quietly broke down.

A D1 athlete
with knees that screamed
and a smile that stayed fixed—
because no one could ever know
how close I was to crumbling.

I lost sleep.
Lost softness.
Lost girlhood.
But I never lost my drive—

even when it drove me
into the ground.

Looking back,
maybe I didn't get sick.
Maybe I was already sick.
Sick from over-functioning.
Sick from striving.
Sick from being the strong one
for too long.

And my body—
brilliant and tired—
finally said,
"If you won't slow down, I'll make you."

I didn't choose the gift,
but I chose the grind.
Because when you're chosen,
you think sacrifice is required.
And maybe it was.

But what I didn't know
was what it would cost:
The birthdays missed.
The laughs skipped.
The quiet ache
of watching the world play
while I worked.

They say stress is silent.
But it screamed through me
in tension headaches,

tight throats,
numb hands,
a body begging for rest
and a soul that forgot how.

And yet—
somehow, I'm still here.
Not perfect.
But real.
Not empty.
But finally full of me.

~

Reflection Prompt: *The Cost of Being "The Gifted One"*

- What did you lose to perfectionism—and what are you ready to reclaim?
- Can you remember a time you punished yourself for not getting it *"just right"*? What did you need in that moment instead?
- What would it look like to honor your talent without tying your worth to it?
- Who were you before you were *"the responsible one"*? Do you still carry her?
- What messages about success, strength, and survival have you outgrown—and what truths are you finally ready to live by?

Clockwork

for the ones surviving in silence, one pill at a time

Dear Fellow Warrior,
Your strength isn't only in survival—
it's in your willingness to feel,
to endure, to hope,
even in the quiet, aching in-between.
You are carrying more than most will ever know,
and still, you remain.

I sit surrounded by bottles,
reading labels I barely understand,
swallowing names like strangers:
Naproxen, Diclofenac, Oxycodone…

Pills.
Pills.
Pills.

Each pill a battle,
each dose a step down a cancerous aisle,
a quiet fight in a war no one sees.

At first, it felt strange—
this invasion of my body by chemicals,
the sharp taste of medicine,
the dizzy haze that followed.

But over time,
I've grown used to the numbness— the dulling of sharp
edges, the softening of pain's harsh outlines.

I've thought about those who swallow pills for other
reasons— not for healing a body broken by disease,
but to numb hearts broken by life.

Those pills that dull grief, anxiety, loneliness,
the life cancer no scan can detect.

Sometimes I wonder— if the numbness I'm learning to
live with is a refuge or a prison.

A quiet place where pain can't find me,
or a fog that steals away the colors of life—
joy, sorrow, rage, and love.

They take their pills
like clockwork— a ritual in surviving,
a small shield against the sharp edge of hours.

They pour their drinks
like holy water— a ritual in forgetting,
the only way to dull the sting of time.

But life looms heavy,
its weight unchanged.
The world keeps spinning,
forgetting how to care,
while they sit still,
swallowing silence
with water and willpower.

Sometimes, it's enough.
Sometimes, it's not.
They're still here—
an accomplishment in itself.

The pills I take fight a known enemy,
but their side effects echo the silent battles
we all face—
the unseen weight,
the quiet despair,
the numbness that becomes ritual.

I've come to understand this numbness—
its double edge cutting through my days.
It shields me from pain's fiercest blows,
but sometimes it steals the feeling of being alive—
the laughter,
the tears,
the very breath of living.

I'm learning how to live in that space—
to find my voice inside the quiet,
to hold onto hope
when the colors fade to gray.

How does one dance with despair
and still hear joy in the music?
How can a heart hold
both sorrow and song
without shattering?

We all sip from sorrow,
searching for sweetness
that might remain.

Dear Fellow Warrior,
whether your fight is marked by medicine bottles,
or by the invisible burdens you carry—
you are not alone.

We swallow our rainbows—
each pill, each breath, each day—
a quiet act of courage,
a testament to survival.

~

Reflection Prompt: *Dancing with the Gray*

- How do you experience the *"numbness"* in your own life?
- When does it protect you, and when does it hold you back?
- What small acts of courage help you reconnect with the colors of living, even when the world feels gray?
- What does survival look like for you on a quiet day—without applause, without witness?

Weathering the Storm

for the ones baptized by chaos and born again in clarity

Dear Fellow Warrior,
You've stood in the downpour
and still didn't drown.
This poem is about the kind of strength
that doesn't look heroic,
but endures.
That's the power
of a Warrior
who refuses to be washed away.

    I been through storms
    that didn't just rattle windows—
    they split me open.
    Didn't just shake my roof—
    they rearranged my soul.
    Lightning didn't just strike—
    it etched scripture into my bones.
    Thunder didn't just roll—
    it rattled my ribcage
    like a war cry from the divine.

    I used to pray for mercy.
    For quiet.
    For clear skies.
    But now I know—
    the storm ain't always punishment.
    Sometimes, it's permission.

Permission to fall apart.
To weep. To bleed.
To be still enough to hear God's voice in the wind.

Because storms?
They don't just destroy— they unmask.
They reveal the weak seams in strong faces.
They peel back pride
and expose the places
where you built with performance
but not with peace.
Where your roots ran shallow.
Where your faith was fancy—
but not fortified.

And you... Yes, you—
drenched in doubt,
barefoot in the aftermath,
still breathing...

Don't you know?
Your survival is a sermon.
Your presence, a praise report.

The storm didn't come to bury you.
It came to baptize you.
To cleanse you of what couldn't come with you
into your next becoming.

You are not broken.
You are breaking open.
And that difference?

That's the difference between death…
and destiny.

So hold on.
To hope. To heart.
To the hem of what's holy.

Let the wind wail.
Let the sky split.
Let the chaos speak.

Because you are not the storm—
but you are storm-born.
Carved by the crashing.
Tempered by the tearing.

You rise,
not in spite of the pain—
but because of it.

This— This is how diamonds form.
How prophets are made.
How legacy is birthed
in the wreckage and the resurrection.

So when the clouds return—
and they will—
don't run.
Raise your arms like branches.
Let the heavens open.
Let it come.
Let it cleanse you.
Let it crown you.

Because you—
child of thunder,
keeper of sacred fire—
you don't just weather the storm.
You become it.
And still—
you shine.

~

Reflection Prompt: *Storm-Born Strength*

- When have you faced a storm—emotionally, spiritually, or physically—that changed you?
- What truths surfaced through that chaos?
- How did you rebuild, and what did you leave behind?
- In what ways have your most difficult experiences forged your power?

Held Hostage by the Start (and still trying anyway)

for the quiet fighters, the dreamers stuck in place, and the ones learning to start again

Dear Fellow Warrior,
Some days, the bravest thing you can do

is simply choose to try again.
No one tells you how heavy survival feels
when the world stops clapping.
This poem honors the sacred stillness between storms—
the ache that lingers after the light fades,
and the courage it takes to start again
when your heart is still sore.
You don't have to move mountains today.
You just have to remember:
even here,
you are worthy.

At 8:11 a.m.
I lie awake.
Breathing shallow, not out of peace,
but pressure.
Tossing. Turning.
Same as I did at 8:11 p.m.,
twelve hours before.
Since then, I've been awake—
body still, but mind sprinting.

My thoughts used to taste like hunger—
passion, dreams, fire in my chest.
But now they feel like blame.
Like maybe my ambition
is what cracked me open.
Like maybe chasing excellence
is what ran me into the ground.

How did I get here?
Twenty-one and diagnosed,

wondering if the way I moved through the world
forced my body to slow me down.
What if this pause isn't healing—
but punishment?

I made magic before I knew the cost.
Sewed until my fingers cramped.
Smiled until my jaw ached.
Climbed ladders while bleeding,
and told myself that was strength.

Now the silence roars louder than the crowds ever did.
After the fashion show,
after the interviews,
after the applause—
came the stillness.
And I couldn't tell
if it was peace
or grief
or guilt
or all three at once.

I tried everything they said:
Meditation. Movement.
Affirmations like armor.
But the low still came.
The ache behind my eyes
and between my ribs
screamed louder than my passion ever could.

This is what no one tells you—
That rest can feel like failure

when you were raised on dreams.
That stillness can feel like surrender
when your gift once felt like oxygen.

I want to keep going.
I want to keep building.
But how do you chase legacy
when your body is begging you
to just survive?
How do you push
when you now know
what pushing too hard can do?

I don't have the answers.
But I do have breath.
And for now—
that's enough.

So I return
to what has always saved me:
My pen.
My prayers.
My pulse.

Maybe I won't launch the next thing today.
Maybe I'll just make tea.
Do my self care
Write one line.
Rest.
Not as a retreat—
but as resistance.

Because even here,
in the ache,
in the aftermath,
I am not a failure.
I am still becoming.

~

Reflection Prompt: *When the Hustle Becomes a Question*

- What dreams have driven you—and have they ever cost you your health or peace?
- Can you recall a moment where your passion became pain?
- How do you reconcile ambition with the need for rest, healing, and boundaries?
- What would it look like to pursue your purpose without losing yourself?
- Write a letter to the version of you who believed success required suffering. What does she need to hear now?

Dear Fellow Warrior: A Two-Part Letter

for the ones still fighting, and the ones still waiting

Dear Fellow Warrior,
You are not just surviving— you are becoming.
This poem is a reflection of the quiet strength it takes to transform in the midst of the storm— and a love letter to the next Warrior waiting to rise.

Part I: While You Are Still in It

I didn't always feel like a Warrior.
Most days, I felt like a ghost in my own skin—
a stranger beneath the hospital gowns,
beneath the wigs,
beneath the weight of *"be strong."*

The fight began quietly.
No sword. No armor.
Just trembling hands
and the hum of fluorescent lights
in a doctor's office
where the world shifted without warning.

I lost more than hair.
I lost pieces of myself
I never knew I held so tightly—
my confidence,
my rhythm,
my reflection.

And still, I smiled.
Because the world didn't need to know.
Because I wanted to be normal,

to walk through life without the pity
that sticks like glue to a diagnosis.

So I hid.
Tucked my pain beneath scarves and silence.
Tried to make myself smaller
so the sickness wouldn't take up all the space.

But oh, fellow Warrior—
I see you.
I see the brave way you breathe
even when it hurts.
I see the courage it takes
just to show up,
just to keep moving,
even if no one claps when you do.

I see the tears you cry
in bathrooms and bedrooms,
the prayers you whisper
not for healing—
but for peace,
for sleep,
for one good day.

This journey is brutal.
Unforgiving.
And too often, unseen.

But you are not invisible to me.
You are not your thinning lashes
or your slow steps
or your quiet withdrawals from the life you once led.

You are not the girl you were before—
You are the Warrior rising in her place.

And no one tells you this part:
that even in the battle,
you are blooming.
Even in the breaking,
you are becoming.

You are not weak for being tired.
You are not less for needing rest.
You are not a burden—
you are a battlefield
and a blooming garden
all at once.

Dear Fellow Warrior,
keep holding on.
Keep reaching for small joys.
Keep showing up for yourself,
even if it's just to cry,
to rest, to breathe.

There is light ahead.
Not just survival— but freedom.
Not just healing— but wholeness.

And when you get there,
when you look back on this storm
and see how far you've come,
you'll know:
You weren't just fighting.
You were transforming.

You were becoming
the kind of woman
who gives hope to the next Warrior.
The kind of woman
writing poems like this one.

With all my heart,
and all my scars,
and all my love,
I see you.
You are not alone.

~

Part II: For the Girl Still Waiting

To the girl sitting in the waiting room,
clutching her wrists like a lifeline,
wondering if anyone sees her—
I do.
I see you. I was you.
And I've made it through
just far enough to turn around
and reach my hand back.

You don't have to do this alone anymore.
The world is still heavy, yes—
but you've got sisters now.
Women like me
who will not let you disappear
into your diagnosis.

Who will speak your name
with tenderness and truth.

This is your invitation
to come out of hiding.
To sit beside me
when your hope feels too small.
To cry, to cuss, to collapse— and still be loved.
Still be held.
Still be worthy.

We're building something different now.
A world where softness and survival coexist.
Where your story isn't too much.
Where your scars don't disqualify you—
they connect you.

So come.
Bring your anger.
Bring your ache.
Bring the version of you that feels hard to carry.
You don't have to be brave here.
You just have to be.

This is your safe space.
I made it for *you*.

And if no one else told you today:
You are already enough.
You are already loved.
You are already home.

~

Reflection Prompt: *For the Girl Still Waiting*

- In your toughest moments, what small acts of courage keep you moving forward?
- How do you see yourself as both Warrior and healer?
- What do you wish someone had said to you in your darkest hour?
- If you wrote a letter to your younger self—or a girl still waiting—what would it say?
- What would it feel like to become the safe space you've always needed?

II. The Crawl Toward Clarity

The Caterpillar — Stillness, Grief, and Growing Pains
When becoming means undoing who you thought you had to be.

The caterpillar doesn't burst into beauty.
It crawls—soft, slow, unseen.
It doesn't know it's preparing for wings.
It only knows hunger—for more, for enough,
for anything that will keep it alive through the ache.

This is the season where growth feels like grief.
Where you shed version after version
of who you were told to be,
and none of it fits anymore.

You've emerged from the rupture—
the diagnosis, the heartbreak, the unraveling.
And now you are here, in the quiet in-between.

No longer who you were,
not yet who you will become.

Stillness becomes your sanctuary—
not because you choose it,
but because your soul demands it.
Because the world got loud,
and your body got tired,
and something deep inside whispered: **stop.**

Here, in the crawl, you are allowed to move slowly.
To rest. To retreat.
To protect your softness
while everything inside you learns a new shape.

The world won't clap.
Won't post your progress.
Won't understand your silence—
but you will keep going anyway.

For me, the crawl meant
running my business full-time
while quietly battling for my life.
Only my innermost circle knew.
I kept creating in secret.
Pushing when my body said no—
not out of denial, but defiance.
Because somewhere between pain and purpose,
I believed I could stitch myself whole again.

Maybe you're there too—
grieving what was, uncertain of what's next.
You are not broken. You are in process.
And the process is sacred.

This is not the end.
This is *the crawl toward clarity.*

Overnight Woman

*for the girl who returned home changed—and chose to
stay free*

Dear Fellow Warrior,
*Some moments force you to grow up in a blink.
This poem captures the instant everything changed—
when innocence turned to survival, and you learned how
to carry your own name with fire.
Let this be a mirror and a map—for the woman you
were, the one you are becoming, and the Warrior rising
from the ache.*

I came home different.
Same bed, same walls—
but I'd outgrown the girl
who painted her world pink and purple.
She was light before the storm.
Now I moved through the hallway
like a stranger in a place
that once knew my name.

Growth didn't ask permission.
It came overnight—
in IVs and diagnosis,
in fears that found no answers.
And suddenly,
my childhood bedroom
felt like a museum
to a person I used to be.

Back under my mother's roof,
but not the same daughter.
College gave me wings—
then illness clipped them.
Her love was everywhere—
but so was her worry.
And it suffocated.

I needed space to breathe,
room to hurt out loud
without being wrapped in panic.
Hard truths stayed stuck
in the throat of the non-confrontational girl
I used to be.
But silence served no one.

Sometimes the greatest act of love
is saying,
This doesn't feel like love right now.
And sometimes, the most radical peace we can offer
is the truth we've been afraid to speak.

So I took it all down—
posters, pictures, past versions of me.
Blank walls felt safer
than a shrine to a self
I no longer recognized.
I gave things away—
closet to Goodwill,
heart to healing.

Because sometimes
you have to release pieces of your past
to make space for who you're becoming.

Helping others helped me, too.
There's power in generosity
even when you're running on empty.
Change doesn't ask if you're ready—
only if you're willing.

The show ended. The silence hit harder than the
applause. No next event—just reality,
loud in its stillness.

I tried to outrun the ache, but it stayed— Familiar,
but not final.

Mental health is not a luxury— It's survival.
And some days, the bravest thing I do is say **NO**.

No to people who drain more than they pour.
No to versions of me that prioritize peacekeeping
over peace of mind.

When my motivation fades,
I reach inward.
When my faith feels faint,
I speak to myself like someone I love.

Because self-destruction
starts with small dismissals of self.
But healing begins
the moment you put yourself
back at the center.

Reflection Prompt: *The Shift, the Silence, and the Self*

- When have you felt suddenly changed, as if you returned to a familiar place but were no longer the same?
- How do you navigate the tension between receiving care and needing space?
- What parts of your past have you released to create room for healing and growth?
- After a high point or breakthrough, how do you hold yourself through the quiet aftermath?
- What boundaries are asking to be honored as a sacred act of self-respect?

Welcome Home (Just As You Are)

for the one who needed permission to rest, to rise, and to receive love

---

Dear Fellow Warrior,
This piece is a sacred offering—
an act of radical tenderness.
It speaks to the deep healing required
when love meets weariness,
especially for those carrying the weight
of generational pain, masculinity, and racial injustice.
This is about loving someone back into wholeness.

About making your presence their peace.
About reminding them:
You are already enough.
You are already home.

Lie down.
Relax.
Let me patch up your daily cracks.
The wrinkles on your forehead
tell me all I need to know.
I can trace those worry lines
into the deep roots of your soul.

First I untie your shoes—
untangling the emotions bottled up inside of you.
As I massage your feet,
my hands release the generational pride
that causes you to drag them.
Stubborn to a fault,
but it's not your own.
Did you hear me?
It's not your fault.

Muscle knots the size of stereotypes
live in your calves— tension from outrunning
expectations
you never agreed to carry.
You don't have to run any further.

I place a kiss on each of your knees,
to soften the prayer bruises
you won't allow to heal.

The ones pressed into midnight conversations with God,
the ones you hope He hears.
He does.

I run my hands up your thighs.
Tears falls from my eyes—
I can feel the power you hold in them,
stifled by being a Black man in America.
It's okay to skip leg day today, *my love.*

When I kiss your hips,
I press my support into the joints—
a reminder that you don't have to carry it all alone.
I'm always here when you need me.

Soft kisses past your navel and up your torso,
I fill this frame with my love.
I press my ear to your heart
until our bodies beat as one.

When I kiss your shoulders,
I release the burdens.
The injustice. The grief.
Be free, my king.
Adjust your crown.

At your neck,
I take my time.
Encouraging you to dare—
to speak up,
to stand out,
to let your truth spill from your mouth
without fear.

Your voice matters.
You matter.

When my lips meet yours,
it's the first time every time.
Spill your soul into mine.
I can handle it.

My lips move gently around your face—
this face that holds so much magic.
You are my safe place.
And I can be yours too…
if you let me.

Last but not least,
I take your head in my arms.
Disarm.
I'll take it from here.
No harm can reach you when I am near.

As your naked Black body lies before me—
fragile and vulnerable—
I wonder how anyone
could look at you and see anything
but God.

You are magical.
Extraordinary.
A breathtaking view.
I will protect you.

~

Because sometimes clarity doesn't come through
pushing— it comes through pause.
Through tenderness.
Through being held, just as you are.

This poem isn't just about romance—
it's about permission.
To rest. To receive.
To let softness be part of your survival.

In the caterpillar stage,
we don't bloom—we learn to be still.
To let go of the armor that kept us alive
but is now too heavy to carry.
We learn that vulnerability
isn't the opposite of strength—
it is strength.

So whether this love is one that you offer to another,
or the one you are learning to offer yourself—
remember this:
Even here,
heading into the cocoon of your becoming,
you are already worthy
of being welcomed home.

~

Reflection Prompt: *You Are Home*

- When have you felt safe enough to lay down your burdens in the presence of another?

- What does it mean to truly welcome someone—not just into your space, but into your spirit?
- What are three truths about your worth that you want to remember today?
- How can you show someone (or yourself) love that affirms, not fixes?

Beauty Standards

for the girl who stopped shrinking and started shining

Dear Fellow Warrior,
This poem dismantles the lies we've swallowed.
It's a reclamation of beauty in all its forms—
raw, imperfect, authentic.
You don't need to shrink to be seen.
You are one of a kind.

They told me beauty was a crown—
delicate, expensive, earned.
But it was never made for heads like mine.
Too textured. Too deep. Too Black.

I was taught to compete with girls
who didn't look like me.
To see their beauty as the standard—
and mine as deviation.

I straightened my curls,
softened my voice,
learned to survive the mirrors
that only showed me pieces to fix.

My body became a battlefield—
something to shrink, smooth, lighten.
They told me to *"glow up,"*
but only if I glowed like *them*.

Meanwhile, they stole our slang,
our lips, our hips, our soul—
and sold it back to us
without credit.

We were the blueprint—
but never the poster.
Praised in parts,
rarely in full.

But I got tired of hiding.
Tired of editing.
Tired of apologizing
for being the original.

So I picked up the clippers.
Hair already falling in clumps,
fingers trembling with grief and rage.
I had clung to the last strands
as if they were proof I still belonged—
as if losing them meant losing myself.

But I met my own eyes in the mirror,
and said: **Enough.**

With every stroke,
I shed years of shame.
Stripped away the story
that said my worth grew from my hair.
Tears fell freely—
not out of grief,
but liberation.

This wasn't about losing beauty.
It was about redefining it.

Because beauty, real beauty,
is not what fits in a filter
or pleases the crowd.
It's how you hold yourself
when you've been broken.
It's the courage to start again
without apology.
It's the love you extend inward
before anyone else gets to weigh in.

My parents stood beside me,
clippers in hand, tears on cheeks.
And in that moment,
they didn't mourn the little girl I used to be—
they honored the woman I had become.

I finally understood:
I was never meant to meet standards.
I was made to set my own.

And in the eye of the beholder
whose gaze matters most— my own—
I am more than beautiful.
I am free.

~

F.Y.I

And in case you needed a reminder:
You are special. One of a kind.
A work of art.
A spark of light.
A soul that's rare,
a spirit so divine.

The world is better with you in it.
You are enough,
more than you'll ever know.
I wish you could see yourself
through the lens of love—
a reflection of beauty that never ends.

So hold your head high.
Let your spirit shine.
You were made with purpose,
by divine design.

No need to change.
No need to hide.
You're already magic—
just as you are.

Reflection Prompt: *Redefining the Mirror*

- How have societal beauty standards shaped the way you see yourself?
- Are there parts of your identity or appearance you've muted to feel more accepted?
- What would it look like to define beauty on your own terms—from the inside out?
- What would it mean to let go of old stories and claim your reflection as enough, exactly as it is?

The Anchor Within

for the Warrior who learned to steady herself

Dear Fellow Warrior,
In chaos, what holds you?
This piece is an invitation to examine your roots—
the truths that ground you,
the loves that steady you,
the inner voice that won't let you drift too far.

When the storm came,
I reached for hands that never reached back.
Poured my heart into empty cups
and wondered why I still felt thirsty.

I was searching for an anchor in people—
hoping someone would steady me,
mirror me,
match the weight of my love.

But when the waves hit hardest,
they drifted.
And I was left
with only myself—
and the things I make with my hands.

So I turned to creating.
To the hum of my sewing machine,
to the quiet courage of thread pulling through fabric,
to the blank page that never judged me.
My pen moved,
and I felt seen.
My needle pierced silk,
and I remembered I was soft but sharp.

My anchor wasn't a person.
It was a practice.
It was the stillness of making something beautiful
while my world was falling apart.
The first cut of fabric
was a breath I didn't know I was holding.
The glide of ink
was a balm for the bruises they couldn't see.

I stitched my strength,
wrote my release,
sketched my survival.

Each creation a reminder:
you are still here.
You are still you.
Even when no one comes through.

I once thought anchoring meant holding on
to someone else.
But real anchors root you within.

And now—
when frustration rises,
when grief knocks without warning—
I return to my little world.
A universe stitched from imagination,
poetry and purpose.

Here,
in this sacred space I've built
with thread and fire,
I don't just survive.
I soar.

What is your anchor, *Dear Warrior?*
When the world forgets your name—
what do you hold on to
that holds you right back?

~

Reflection Prompt: *Rooting in Practice*

- What anchors you when life feels unsteady?

- Is it a practice, a passion, a ritual, or a quiet corner of your soul?
- How often do you return to it—and how do you feel afterward?
- What would it look like to intentionally nurture this inner sanctuary?
- What could shift in your life if you allowed that space to hold you full?

The Ferry Back to Me

for the woman learning to break before she flies

Dear Fellow Warrior,
This is the part no one talks about.
The in-between. The unraveling.
Where your silence grows too loud,
and your spirit aches to be heard.
This is not the flight—this is the crawl.
But even here, you are healing.

I've longed to disappear—
to drift into sunlight,
to vanish beyond the noise,
to find a place where the ache quiets.
I tried everything they said:
movement, meditation,
hope in small rituals.
Still, the low came.

I ran out of tears.
They swelled behind tired eyes.
I told myself,
I'm a strong Black woman.
And we don't cry.
Right?

But I was always on the verge—
this close to breaking open.
My insides an avalanche
while I smiled through the storm.
No one could know
how weak I felt,
how heavy silence can be
when it's dressed in strength.

Then came the blur—
mornings where breath barely rose,
body sunken into the mattress.
Eyes crusted at the corners.
And still, something stirred.

A little fly danced against the window—
alone, persistent,
fighting for the light.
And I saw myself in her.

The world saw me dancing through life,
I saw myself on the wrong side of my dreams.
I was seemingly twirling through life,
but actually stuck.
Desperate for escape.
Hungry to feel whole.

So I returned— to the one place that always held me
without asking me to perform.
Martha's Vineyard.

Where peace is sewn into the tides,
and the sun rises with intention.
Where the girl I left behind
still wandered the bike paths
with poems in her pocket.

I packed light—
left behind doubt, comparison,
the ache of not being enough.
Boarded the boat like a seeker,
not a guest.
The water greeted me
like a lifelong friend—
choppy, certain, cleansing.

Each wave slapped the hull
like a truth I'd tried to bury.
The Island—my sanctuary,
my soul's best-kept secret—
rose to meet me.

I remembered:
At eleven, I wrote beside the ocean
like it was listening.
And maybe it was.

My mother told stories
of wild nights and summer friends,
of music in the park,
and dancing until dark.
Her adventures were loud—
sun-drunk, pulsing with movement.
Mine were quieter,
a slow unfolding of self.

I used to envy that—
longing for connections

I couldn't seem to make.
But now I see:
what I discovered here
wasn't a crowd.
It was me.

My grandparents,
planted our roots here.
And now, each step I take
is part of their prayer.
Part of their dream.

Here, I became my own best friend.
Here, I learned solitude is sacred.
That softness is not weakness.
That healing can be quiet.
That clarity doesn't come loud—
it comes slowly.
In whispers. In waves.

I don't sleep through the ferry ride anymore.
I stand on the back deck,
watching the shore slip away,
watching the girl I was
reach for the woman I'm still becoming.

Because this isn't just about surviving cancer.
It's about forgiving myself.
Unpacking the weight I was told to carry quietly.

I finally hear it— the sound of my heart weeping,
louder than my silence.
And I no longer turn away.

I sit with her—my aching heart—
and I choose not to abandon her.
I let the grief speak.

I let the old wounds rise.
And still— I stay.
Step by step,
wave by wave,
line by line,
I crawl toward clarity.

~

Reflection *Prompt: Crawling Toward Clarity*

- What emotions have you been taught to hide in the name of strength?
- Where do you go—physically or spiritually—when you need to feel safe again?
- What is one truth you're ready to face, even if it shakes you?
- What might it look like to stay with your heart instead of escaping it?

Reflection

for the Warrior who sees herself through the eyes of her ancestors

---

Dear Fellow Warrior,
Sometimes, the mirror shows us more than our features— it reveals who we are becoming. This is a love note to the brave act of pausing, looking within, and

recognizing the strength that lives just beneath the surface.

Sitting on an empty shore at high tide,
sunken into the rich soil where my ancestors lie.
Held with honor by the sand's warm embrace,
watching the water swell around my exhausted body.

Welcoming in every drop of water
as if I was a plant,
a beautiful blossoming flower.
Stretching toward the sun with silent longing,
feeling grateful for a place of belonging—here.

Rooted deep within the marrow of my being,
I fill my mind with thoughts of gratitude,
pouring into my soul in multitudes.
Like rain quenching a centuries-old thirst,
I fill my cup with tenacity.
I fill my cup with distinction.
I fill my cup with the eternal well of wisdom.

I reclaim my time on this earth with my worth.
I reclaim my right to obtain what is justifiably mine.
I will continue to build this kingdom
within and without—
with building legacy at the forefront of my mind,
no doubts.

As I recite these words aloud,
sending them out into the universe,
I lie back and submerge my body
into the Inkwell's sanctified waters.

The rhythmic whispers of the waves fill me.
The chant of my words heal me.
Their hands—
forged from earth—
resonating with revitalizing echoes.

My ancestors have lifted me up,
yet again.
Allowing me to release what no longer serves me.

Revitalizing echoes—
evoking this deep, ancestral wisdom
that's not just remembered,
but felt in the body.
There's a kind of cleansing and empowerment
happening *here*.

~

Reflection Prompt: *Remembering You Are Your Ancestors Dreams*

- How do you connect with your roots and ancestral strength?
- What legacy do you carry in your bones—and how does it speak through you?
- What practices ground you in gratitude and remind you of your power?
- What are you ready to release in order to rise more fully?
- What part of you needs to be seen, heard, and honored today?

From Stigma to Strength

for the ones choosing to heal, even when it's hard

Dear Fellow Warrior,
Choosing to seek help is an act of courage and self-love— especially when silence and stigma have tried to keep us small.
You are not alone in this journey.
Your healing matters, and your story deserves to be held with care.

Last week I signed up for therapy—
Today is my first appointment.
I walked in, heart pounding,
palms sweaty, mind blank,
caught between wanting to speak
and fearing vulnerability.

Sharing my story with a stranger,
the weight of stigma pressing—
therapy, still whispered about
in hushed tones behind closed doors,
especially in Black and Brown rooms,
where strength is survival,
and asking for help, a sign of weakness.

But here I am,
breaking that silence,
choosing courage over comfort,
deciding my mental health
is worth the fight.

Anxiety, trauma, boundaries—
imposter syndrome that whispers,
"You're not enough."
The stories we carry,
woven with doubt and pain,
but also resilience, hope, and power.

This space is for me—to explore,
to name the wounds no one sees,
to unlearn shame,
to rewrite my narrative.

Because healing is revolutionary.
Self-love is radical.
And growth begins when we
show up honestly,
even when it's hard.

Dear Fellow Warrior,
therapy isn't a weakness—
it's a gift, a lifeline,
a mirror held with kindness.

If you've held back,
if you've been taught to hide,
know this:

Your story deserves to be heard.
Your wounds deserve care and attention.

Take the first step.
Make the list.
Start the conversation.

Because in seeking help,
we are in fact reclaiming our power—
not just for ourselves,
but for every soul waiting to be freed from silence.

Break the stigma.
Heal. Rise.

~

Reflection Prompt: *Reclaiming Healing*

- What fears or beliefs have kept you from seeking support for your mental health?
- How might your life change if you embraced therapy as a tool for strength and growth?
- What internalized messages about *"being strong"* are you ready to release?
- What small step can you take today to honor your emotional well-being?

When Faith Meets the Mirror

for the moments when belief feels just out of reach

Dear Fellow Warrior,
In the moments when doubt feels heavier than hope,
remember:
Faith is not always loud or certain.
It is a quiet, brave choice
to keep walking even when the path is dark.
You are not alone in your struggle—
your courage to believe and to keep going
is a victory in itself.

There was a time
I wasn't sure
if anyone—
even God—
was listening.

I wasn't raised in pews
or sanctuaries on a consistent basis,
but I always believed in something higher.
My grandparents' faith
was stitched into every word they spoke—
a soft kind of knowing
passed down like prayer.
And I tried—
honestly, I tried—
to follow the thread.

I was baptized at Trinity Episcopal Church
in Oak Bluffs,
where my grandfather built his legacy on the Island.
Sometimes, I'd return
just to sit on the bench
we placed in his honor—
outside the church,
a sacred pause.
I'd close my eyes,
breathe deep,
and hope to channel his wisdom.

But belief isn't borrowed.
It must be built.

So I began seeking—
walking into churches
with quiet courage,
sitting in back rows,
searching for home.
I lit prayers like candles,
whispered gratitude in the dark,
and waited.

Then came the storm.
The diagnosis.
The ache.
The fear.

And with it—
questions I didn't know I had:
Why me?

Where are You?
Are You even real?

The doubt felt heavier
than the disease.
I stood at a crossroads—
one path, dark
and hopeless.
The other,
lit only
by the flicker
of fragile faith.

So I made a choice:
to *let go and let God.*
Even when it didn't make sense,
I kept praying.
Even when I wasn't sure,
I kept believing.
Not because I was certain—
but because walking alone
felt colder than doubt itself.

Sometimes,
there is no reason.
No karma.
No punishment.
No hidden lesson.

We break ourselves searching for one.
We shrink, asking, *"Why me?"*

We ache, thinking we deserved it.
We rage. We retreat.

But here's the truth:
Not everything is your fault.
And not everything is meant to be fixed.
Some things, are simply meant to be faced.

So be soft with yourself.
Be gentle.
Wrap your arms around your own heart—
not out of pity, but out of love.

Because even when life breaks you,
you still get to choose:
Will I fight?
Will I believe?
Will I love myself enough to keep going?

I hope you say yes.
I did.

~

Reflection Prompt: *Faith in the Face of Fear*

- When have you stood at a crossroads between doubt and faith?
- How do you nurture hope when answers are absent or unclear?
- What does surrender look like in your life—and how has it led to unexpected peace or healing?

- How might softness toward yourself become a new form of strength?
- Where do you turn when life becomes too heavy to carry alone?

III. The Quiet Metamorphosis

The Chrysalis — Confined but Transforming
Where healing happens in silence, and transformation takes root unseen

---

You were no longer crawling,
but you couldn't yet fly.
So you went inward.
Not to hide—but to heal.
Not to disappear—but to transform.

From the outside, it looked like stillness.
But inside, everything was changing.
Grief pressed against your ribs.
Loneliness sat heavy.
But under it all,
something sacred stirred.

Your body was still aching.
Your heart, still tender.
But your spirit?
Your spirit was sharpening its edges.

You began to stitch meaning into your scars.
To name your pain out loud.
To whisper *"no"* and **mean it.**
To stop shrinking to be chosen
and start expanding to be whole.

This was the unbecoming—
of perfection, of performance,
of every version of you that survived but never thrived.

It was not glamorous.
There were no cameras.
No clapping.
Only the holy work of becoming.

In the chrysalis, the caterpillar dissolves completely.
Nothing recognizable remains.
But within that breakdown
is the blueprint for wings.

You stayed.
You chose therapy, rest,
boundaries, truth.
You dared to believe that softness was not weakness,
that solitude was not abandonment,
that silence could be a sanctuary.

You didn't bloom in public.
You bloomed in the dark.
And that, *Dear Warrior,*
was your *quiet metamorphosis.*

Boundaries Like Breath, Like Armor

for the one learning that "NO" is sacred

Dear Fellow Warrior,
Not everyone is meant to access your softness.
This is about the sacred power of saying no,
of protecting your peace like your life depends on it—
because sometimes, it does.
Boundaries aren't walls.
They're breath. They're armor.
They're a full-bodied prayer
to never abandon yourself again.

    Mental health is not a luxury—
    it's *survival.*
    And some days,
    the bravest thing I do
    is say no.
    No to people
    who drain more than they pour.
    No to versions of me
    that prioritize peacekeeping
    over peace of mind.

    When my motivation fades,
    I reach inward.
    When my faith feels faint,

I speak to myself
like someone I love.

Because self-destruction
starts with small dismissals of self.
But healing begins
the moment you put yourself
back at the center.

"Common sense is not so common."
—My mother used to say.

People will always have something to say—
Especially about things that don't concern them.
Your body, your choices, your healing.
With flushed cheeks, a bare scalp,
and a soft voice, I was still learning to trust,
I became a magnet for questions I never asked for.

There's this strange entitlement some people carry—
to your story, your spirit, your scars.
But here's the truth:
You don't owe anyone access to your sacred space.
You don't need to shrink yourself to be palatable.
Leave it to others to be intrusive—
Leave it to yourself to be whole.

I used to believe that helping everyone
meant I was kind, loyal—complete.
But I was pouring from a cup already cracked,
offering fragments of myself
to those who had forgotten what they were worth.

Some left silently.
Some stayed too long.
And I mistook history for harmony,
clung to ghosts—
not because I needed them,
but because I couldn't bear
to watch the wind carry off
what once felt like forever.

I've learned—
when you force a connection past its season,
disappointment blooms like clockwork.

So now I pause.
Now I ask: *Does this nourish me,
or does it drain me?*

Boundaries aren't walls.
They are doors with locks
only you can open.
They are soft no's that protect your sacred yes.
They are grace when you've given too much.

I used to betray myself
in the name of being easygoing—
dimmed my needs
to keep the peace,
but lost the war inside.

Now I check in:
*Am I honoring my energy?
Am I standing in my worth?*

Because when I speak up,
even if my voice shakes,
I remind myself:
I am not difficult for having limits.
I am not selfish for needing space.

Some won't understand.
Some will push back.
Some will quietly leave.
Let them.

Boundaries reveal who is here
for you— and who was only here
for your silence.

Not everyone is meant to stay.
That's not cruelty— it's *clarity.*

Every goodbye made room for growth.
Every letting go became a letting in—
of strength,
of stillness,
of me.

I wake now
not asking the day to be perfect—
but asking myself to show up with intention.

Because when I believe I am worthy,
I act like it.
And when I act like it,
my life responds.

Discipline is not punishment—
it is devotion
to the version of me
I promised to become.

You are not hard to love
for having boundaries.
You are not mean
for walking away.
You are not broken
because some chapters closed too soon.

You are a garden—
not everyone deserves to plant there.
And the ones who do
will not flinch
when you bloom.

Breathe deep.
Hold your ground.
Choose you—again and again.
That is not selfish.
That is *sacred*.

~

Reflection Prompt: *The Sacred No*

- What boundary are you being called to honor right now?
- Where in your life are you still choosing comfort over clarity, or guilt over growth?

- What might shift if you gave yourself full permission to say no—with softness and strength?
- Write a list of non-negotiables that keep you rooted in self-respect.

Let one of them guide you this week.

Truth Hurts

for the ones carrying truths too heavy to hold alone

Dear Fellow Warrior,
When the truth finally surfaces,
it doesn't always arrive gently.
This poem holds space for the sting,
the rupture, and the clarity that comes
when we stop shrinking our truth
to make others comfortable.

Before you read this,
breathe.

Not every wound was meant to bleed in public.
Not every truth was meant to be told.
But some truths are too heavy to carry alone—
so I lay them here,
in the open,
hoping you'll still see me whole.

The truth?
We're all a little broken.
We carry shadows deeper than any tunnel,
twisting through thoughts we're too afraid to share.
We suffer for things we never did,
pay for the silence of others,
break beneath a weight we were never meant to bear.

I know we can do better.
That's why I'm writing this letter.

You don't even know the half of it.
And I'm scared—
scared that if you ever knew,
it might break you too.
The battles I fight in silence.
The wounds I've hidden so well.

I pray God holds our hearts together,
keeps them from splitting at the seams
as this world tries to pull us apart.
Because the thought of your spirit breaking—
I can't unsee it.
It's burned into me.

They say if you love someone, let them go.
But if I love you...
should I let you know?

I'm scared of your thoughts,
because I promise you—
mine are darker.

I'm scared you'll run.
That your body will carry you far from me,
galloping toward peace
while I sit in the wreckage I've become.

I hate to say it like this,
but I need you to hear me.
We're drowning in truths
we've both tried to dismiss.

It's time.
To end the cycle.
To speak.
To feel.
To heal.

~

Reflection Prompt: *Truth as a Starting Point*

- What truths are hardest for you to face—about yourself, your relationships, or your past?
- How have you tried to protect others by hiding parts of your truth?
- What healing might begin if you allowed yourself to be fully seen?
- Where in your life could honesty be a doorway, not a rupture?

Dead Weight (The Art of Letting Go)

for the Warrior who carried more than she should have ever had to

---

Dear Fellow Warrior,
You've carried so much for so long.
Some of it was never yours. Some of it was.
But none of it has to define you now.
This is not about forgetting. It's about remembering who you are beneath the heaviness.
This is for the part of you that held pain like it was sacred, that clutched heartbreak like a blueprint for protection.
You cannot heal while dragging what's breaking you.
But release is its own masterpiece— forgiveness its own kind of freedom.
You don't let go to erase the past.
You let go to finally return to yourself.
This is your release story.
This is your rise.

I was eight
when I first learned
how a promise could lie.
How a *"yes"* from my father
could vanish into another weekend
spent waiting by the window.

And I—
a little girl too soft for that kind of disappointment—
learned to wear a grudge like armor.
But still,
I'd throw it aside
every time he came back.
Because I loved him that much.
I thought if I held on tight enough,
he'd stay.
Maybe he'd see
how much I needed him—
how much beauty I saw in the man he was.

Middle school taught me
that joy could be dangerous.
They laughed at my height,
my smile, my voice—
said I was too much,
too proper,
too in-between.
So I stopped caring.
At least, that's what I told myself.

I built a wall
and called it strength.
But really,
it was scar tissue
masquerading as survival.

I loved school,
but bullies made it hard

to walk through those doors
of what once felt like safety.

Love showed up in hunger, not honor—
being touched without tenderness,
wanted but never protected.
I said I forgave them,
but flinched every time
someone called me beautiful—
as if beauty was a warning,
not a wonder.

Friends once called me
"sis forever"— then disappeared
when my storm arrived.
I thought I did something wrong.
But the truth?
I only made the mistake
of thinking they knew how to stay.

So I carried it all—
anger, hurt, betrayal—
stacked them like bricks,
built a home inside my own bitterness.
But I couldn't breathe in there anymore.

Some people dropped off,
and I lost some dead weight.
Funny thing is— I didn't feel lighter.
Just stronger.
Carrying only what serves me.

They didn't see the vision.
So I stopped explaining.
Left them blind to the mission.
Now I move with purpose.
No stress.

People come and go— seasons shift,
but I remain.
And still, I rise.

I rise from betrayal,
from hatred,
from the ashes of love
I once held sacred.

Wishing old friends, lovers,
business partners— good luck.
No hate in my heart,
just peace when I look back.

Truth is—
I wouldn't be here without them.
So thank you,
for the lessons and the losses.

I'm grateful,
through and through.
Wishing you light on your journey
as I shine on mine.
No bitterness, only brilliance—
as we both redefine.

I hope you find what you've been searching for.
And I find peace in knowing
I helped you grow.
I hope you find peace in knowing
you taught me how to let go.

Because forgiveness
has never been my strongest art.
When I love, I love fully—
Naively, with a wide-open heart.

I gave chances,
excuses, doubts—
until one day,
I chose silence as my last goodbye.

Still, I know:
we're human.
Imperfect. Learning.

So I choose mercy.
I extend grace.
I unclench my heart.
I let go.

Forgiveness isn't letting them off the hook.
It's letting me off the leash.
It's saying:
I release you so I can return to myself.

It's the exhale
after years of holding my breath.
Not a finish line— but a daily decision.

To choose peace over punishment.
Grace over grudges.
Growth over ghosts.

Some sadness visits like a thief—
silent and heavy.
But I no longer let it steal my joy.
I look in the mirror and ask:
What must I release
to be free?

Self-belief is a quiet flame.
A reminder that I am enough.
That I can start again—
with boundaries, with breath,
with the art of staying whole.

This is what I know now:
I am not what they did to me.
I am not what I held onto.
I am what I've chosen to release.

I still remember every broken promise—
but I no longer live under their weight.
I live free.

And that— that is the real miracle.

I am not the wound.
I am the healing.
I am not the weight.
I am the rising.

I am not the past.
I am the letting go.

And I am still becoming.

~

Reflection Prompt: *Unclenching the Heart*

- What burdens are you still carrying that no longer belong to you?
- What hurt are you holding out of habit—long after it stopped helping you survive?
- Who have you silently forgiven but never fully released?
- What parts of your past have you outgrown, yet still feel obligated to carry?
- Write two letters:One to the burden—name it, thank it, and say goodbye. One to the version of you who remains after it's gone—stronger, freer, whole.
- What would it feel like to live unburdened—and to believe you truly deserve that kind of peace?

A Cry for Change

for every woman who flinched before she learned to love, and every country still pretending it doesn't see us.

Dear Fellow Warrior,
This poem is an alarm bell.
It was written in grief, in fury,
in the name of every woman buried too soon,
unheard and unheld. A reckoning.
A refusal to play polite in a world that has never
protected us.
If you've ever swallowed your pain
to make someone else comfortable,
this piece is for you.
Let it echo through your bones.
Let it move us beyond pity toward protection.
Let it disrupt comfort,
so something just can begin.

She learned to flinch
before she learned to love.
Read rage before it reached his tongue.
Wore apologies like a second skin—
soft-spoken sorries etched in with purple bruises.

But pain doesn't always shout.
Sometimes, it whispers.
Rewrites your memory
until you mistake control for care,
cages for comfort.

She clipped her own wings
just to survive in the space he gave her.
And the world just watched.
Shrugged.
Said, *"Love is pain."*

And then they ask:
"How are you doing?"
Ten muscles lift a lie across my lips:
"I'm doing good."
But inside, I am on fire.

I carry her bruises in my chest.
I carry their screams in my spine.
Women trafficked.
Girls forced.
Voices silenced.

If I told the truth—
that depression sleeps beside me,
that numbness has started to feel like safety—
they'd offer pity, not change.
They don't want the truth.
They want a version of me
that doesn't disrupt the comfort of their day.

But I think about them—
Black and Brown women
whose backs are breaking
under the weight of generations.
Girls called *women*
before their first bra strap had time to stretch.

Daughters offered to men like sacrifice.
Their no somehow mistranslated
into something softer,
less human.
Their silence mistaken for consent.

Just because it says *"F"* instead of *"M"*
on our birth certificates,
doesn't mean our pain is expected.
Doesn't mean we were born
to be broken.

When they ask how I'm doing,
I think of mutilated genitals,
of stolen educations,
of girls married off like livestock—
with dowries and dead dreams.

I think of my own survival.
Of the disease that tried to rob me quietly,
the pills I take just to move through the day.
And I wonder—
how many women learned to smile through sedation?

There's a kind of comfort in forgetting.
In silence.
But that's not who I am.
That's not who we are.

We are not numb. We are not naive.
Because we've seen America unmasked—
not the version they wrap in red, white, and blue,
but the one that lets women vanish
without asking why.
The one that calls our trauma resilience
and our silence grace.

My grandmother drank tea with trembling hands.
Almost a century lived,

still afraid of shadows that never left.
Still asking if freedom
is anything more than a beautiful lie.

So no—
I'm not okay.
And I won't be,
not until no woman has to flinch
before she learns to love.

They'll say,
"Yes, it's sad... but what can we do?"
We fight. We write. We speak.
We refuse to go numb.
Because silence has never saved anyone.

~

Reflection Prompt: *When the Silence Breaks*

- When was the last time you said *"I'm okay"* when you weren't?
- What parts of your truth have you silenced for someone else's comfort?
- What stories in your community are still being buried?
- What would it look like to tell the whole truth—not just for you, but for the women who couldn't?

Chosen and Never Released

for the one who's tired of waiting, but still hoping

Dear Fellow Warrior,
Some days, the bravest thing you can do
is simply choose to try again.
No one tells you how heavy survival feels
when the world stops clapping.
This poem honors the sacred stillness between storms—
the ache that lingers after the light fades,
and the courage it takes to start again
when your heart is still sore.
You don't have to move mountains today.
You just have to remember:
even here, you are worthy.

Always alone—
no one checks in like I need,
no one lifts me fully.
They take my best,
leave me with their shadows.
Tired of fighting,
of bending, convincing—
maybe closeness was never meant for me.

Selflessness,
a feast for selfish hands.
Always wanting, never receiving—
hope fades into quiet defeat.

But somewhere deep inside,
a quiet flame still burns—
a stubborn spark that whispers:
"You are worthy. You are enough."

Used, discarded,
called only when needed.
Is it wrong to crave a hand that holds tight?
To be chosen and never released?

The right love waits,
worth every moment.
Don't reshape your soul
to fit where you don't belong.
Stand firm. Be you.
Your tribe will hold on— *and never let go.*

And until then,
hold yourself close.
You are your own
fierce, steady home.

~

Reflection Prompt: *The Love You Deserve*

- When have you felt unseen or taken for granted by those around you?
- How can you begin nurturing the love and care you've always deserved—starting with yourself?
- Are you shrinking or reshaping yourself to meet others' expectations?

- What would it look like to stand firm in your truth and let only those who truly see you draw near?
- Who is your tribe, and how can you call them in—through energy, boundaries, or faith?

Live Prey

for the moments when fear tries to claim you

Dear Fellow Warrior,
Fear is not failure—
it's the beginning of bravery.
Let this poem remind you
that every trembling step forward
is a testament to your strength.

They can sniff out my vulnerability from miles away.
They can see my insecurities as if they are on display—
slipping in unnoticed,
blindsided by their attack.
You might as well call me live prey,
because fear, eats my heart out,
without cutting my anxiety any slack.

Devouring my heart,
crumbling my walls,
leaving me laid bare,

for my next internal brawls.
Seeking a means of defense,
wandering in search of belonging,
hoping to find my place in the world.
They cloak themselves in deception,
striking without warning,
sneaking up on you without a sound.
They exist only to hold you captive—
caged in, with no way out.

One day, I looked in the mirror— and didn't recognize
the girl who kept running.

So I stopped. Turned. Faced it.

It's an ongoing cycle.
You have no choice but to face what's ahead.
Refuse to be the victim.
Let your courage be louder than your fears.
The greatness within you is ready to rise.
It's time to remove the disguise.
You are something special—
so start acting like it.

You carry fire in your chest—
not for burning, but for becoming.
So rise like the blaze you are.

Your spirit guides are handing you the torch.
You're stepping into full ownership of your path.
No more shrinking to fit into spaces
that were never meant to hold your light.
Stand tall in your truth—**unapologetically,**

for even the stars had to fight
through darkness to be seen.
You are no different—
born to rise, to lead,
to be free.

~

Reflection Prompt: *Fear as Fuel*

- When has fear disguised itself as protection in your life?
- What parts of you have been preyed upon—and what new strength rose from the wound?
- In what spaces have you been shrinking, and how can you begin to expand?
- What mask are you ready to remove to reveal your true power?
- If your courage had a voice today, what would it tell you to do next?

Divine Womanhood: A Two-Part Poem

for the one softening into her power

Dear Fellow Warrior,
Becoming a woman isn't always soft.

Sometimes it arrives in waves—through desire, heartbreak, awakening, and ache.
You shed innocence like skin, mistake attention for love, mistake love for home.
But eventually, you return—to your body, your truth, your power.
This is a story of that return.
Of learning what to keep, what to release, and what was never yours to carry.
You are not who they touched, left, or forgot.
You are who you chose to become afterward.

Let this poem walk with you through the fire and into your own becoming.
Not perfect. Not pure.

But whole—and finally, yours.

Part I: When the Season Changed

A sensual evolution
into divine womanhood.
It started in summer—
not the calendar kind,
but the kind that hums beneath skin,
where heat curls low in the belly
and everything ripe begins to ache
for touch.

Girlhood shed itself quietly.
Like linen slipping from sun-kissed shoulders,
like night easing its way across the sea.

I didn't even notice at first—
the slow way my laugh deepened,
the way my hips began speaking
before my mouth did,
the way my breath caught
for reasons I never questioned.

And then I did—notice.
How my thighs softened with certainty.
How I began to savor instead of rush.
How I no longer flirted—
I summoned.

My voice became velvet.
My gaze lingered.
I painted my lips with wine-colored secrets
and wore my scent like an invitation
to remember
what a woman's presence could do.

There was no shame,
only surrender.
To silk sheets tangled at midnight,
to mango juice trailing down my chest,
to the low moan of my name
rising off someone's grateful tongue.

The Island taught me—
how to open like hibiscus,
how to press love into every inch of skin,
how to worship myself as thoroughly
as I once wished someone else would.

Now I wear gold hoops and slow jazz.
Oil my thighs with intention.
Walk barefoot in moonlight
and let the night breeze kiss
every grown part of me.

Womanhood is not a destination—
it's a divine unraveling.
A remembering. A return
to the fire in my own hips.
The honey in my own hands.
The ocean in my own yes.

When the season changed,
so did I.
And I will never go back
to frost.

~

Part II: Sex on the Beach

Some heartbreaks are teachers.
Some tides, a cleansing.
even in the wreckage,
you are still worthy of love that's true.

For the lessons you didn't see coming—
and the love that taught you how to return to yourself.

Salt clings to our skin
as we drift into the deep sea,

tangled within the tide's rhythm,
lost in the ocean's sweet heat.

Whispers of deception scatter like sand,
fading into the night's embrace.
As the tide washes away
what passion pretended to be—
gone with the waves.

Faceless, nameless strangers,
etched in memory,
leaving only echoes—
silver-tongued and fleeting,
weightless and meaningless.

Choices made and left behind,
each one still holding weight,
a shadow, a scar.
But in their grasp,
I found my strength—
a lesson learned, a soul redefined.

A rudeboi's touch lingers like salt,
stinging softly long after the waves retreat.

Bruised by counterfeit kisses,
I clawed through thorns of longing

I bled my way to you, *my darling*—

For in the struggle,
I found something greater than romance—

I found discernment.
I found me.

I mistook pleasure for peace,
attention for affection,
proximity for protection.

But now, I know the difference.
I gather the wreckage
not to mourn, but to rebuild.

Because love— true love—
doesn't leave bruises in its wake.
It holds. It heals.

It waits for the version of me
that no longer needs to be rescued.
And maybe that version
is rising now—
from the salt, from the silence,
from the self I once abandoned
just to be chosen.

So if you ask me now
what I've learned from love
that left without staying—
I'd tell you this:
I am not the sum of who hurt me.
I am the woman who kept loving, anyway.

~

Reflection Prompt: *The Rise to Self*

- Where in your life have you confused attention for affection, or presence for protection?
- How have your sensual experiences shaped your understanding of love and self-worth?
- What parts of you bloomed after heartbreak—and how can you honor them now?
- What does it mean to return to yourself fully, without apology or shame?

The Only One Owning It

For the ones who still showed up at the altar of growth

Dear Fellow Warrior,
Accountability is one of the hardest mirrors to stand in front of— especially when you weren't the only one who cracked the glass.
This piece is for the brave-hearted:
the ones who apologize even when it's not reciprocated, the ones who grow in silence, and the ones who carry both the ache of being hurt and the responsibility for how they responded to that hurt.
Healing is messy. But when you know better and still choose better— even without applause— that is where transformation lives.

I said I was sorry
and the silence was louder
than any scream
you'd ever thrown at me.
I held my hands out,
palms up — no weapons,
only the truth.
But truth is a lonely language
when no one else speaks it.
You walked away
still carrying your side of the story
like it was spotless.
Like my apology
was a signed confession
for a crime we both committed.
And maybe I was wrong —
but I was not wrong alone.
Maybe I stayed too long,
bit my tongue too much,
loved too hard
in a place that wasn't safe
for soft things.
I'm not proud
of the ways I failed.
But I faced them.
I named them.
I let them echo in an empty room
where only I showed up to listen.
Accountability feels like exile
when the other person never joins you
at the altar of repair.
But I learned:

healing isn't a shared sentence.
It's a solo vow.
And I'd rather walk alone in truth
than stay surrounded by silence
where no one says a word
about the part they played in the wreckage.

~

Knowing Better

They say,
"When you know better, do better."
But they don't tell you
how heavy the knowing can be—
how it settles in your chest
like wet fabric clinging
to skin you've outgrown.
Growth doesn't feel like glory.
It feels like grief.
Like shedding layers
you once wore with pride.
Like realizing
you weren't just hurt—
you hurt back.
And both can be true.
I know better now.
I know that silence is a response.
That love is not enough
when respect is missing.
That survival tactics
don't work in sacred spaces.

I've learned
to watch my own patterns,
to pause before defending,
to say *"I was wrong"*
without needing to be forgiven.
That's the part no one tells you—
you might never be forgiven.
But still, you choose better.
Because healing is less about
being seen as good,
and more about becoming whole.
And wholeness,
real wholeness—
means loving the parts of you
that broke things,
while still holding yourself
to the standard
of someone who now
knows better.

~

Reflection Prompt: *Compassion and Correction*

- When have you taken responsibility for something that wasn't entirely your fault? How did that feel?
- What truths about yourself have been the hardest to accept — and how have they helped you grow?
- In what ways are you practicing *"doing better"* with the wisdom you've earned?

- How do you honor your own healing when closure or accountability from others never comes?
- Can you hold space for both compassion and self-correction in your journey forward?

If Only She Could See

for the mothers who gave everything— and the children still learning to breathe beyond their expectations to become whole

---

Dear Fellow Warrior,
This poem is a tribute to the fierce, imperfect love between a mother and child— a love forged through sacrifice, struggle, and unspoken battles.
It honors the women who give everything without asking for praise, whose strength often goes unseen, and the complicated emotions that come with holding them both up and holding them accountable. If you carry love mixed with frustration and hope for deeper understanding, this poem is for you.

Dedicated to my mother—
for trying to take my pain away
while carrying her own,
and for the generational curses
she was never meant to break alone.

How did she learn to love me like that—
with a heart that would break
before it let me fall?
To give like rain gives to roots—
not for praise,
but because it's what the earth needs.

How did she pour herself out
until there was nothing left,
and still manage to offer more?

I watched her.
Making something from nothing,
over and over again.
No help.
Just her,
and a will that refused to quit.

She carried us all— on tired legs,
with hands that never stopped giving,
and a heart that stayed soft
even when the world wasn't.

I didn't understand it then.
But I do now— the sacrifices
stitched into our childhood,
the quiet dreams she folded up
so we could chase our own.

She's still just a girl, *really*.
A woman with scars of her own.
A daughter before she became a mother,
doing her best with the information she had.

And I wish—
God, I wish—
she could see herself
the way I see her.
Not through the lens of what she couldn't fix,
but what she fiercely tried to protect.

Sometimes we clash— two strong hearts
speaking different languages
but wanting the same thing:
to be seen.
To be safe.
To be held.

I'm sorry— for holding her to a standard
so high it left no room for her to fall.
For mistaking her love for control
when really, she just wanted to keep me from pain.

But the truth is— she couldn't.
None of them could.
No parent can shield their child
from the path already carved.
From the losses we must live through.
From the breaking that becomes our becoming.

This is what I need her to hear:
You did not fail me.
You loved me with all you had.
But the bloom,
Mama,
has to be mine.

You cannot carry me there.
You cannot control the light,
or the rain, or the storm.
But I thank you— for trying.
For showing up.
For loving me so hard,
it sometimes felt like fear.

I know now—
you were just scared to lose me.
Just like I've been afraid to let you down.

But we're here.
Still holding each other in new ways.
Still learning how to speak softer,
listen longer, let go gently.

You'll always be a part of me—
in my grit, in my giving,
in the way I survive
without letting it harden me.

Your love wasn't perfect.
Neither is mine.
But it's real.
And it's enough.

So maybe— with grace,
with time— we'll find the rhythm
we've both been reaching for.

~

Reflection Prompt: *Grace Between Generations*

- Who in your life embodies the strength, sacrifice, and love described here?
- How has your relationship with them shaped your understanding of love and identity?
- What would it look like to extend grace—to both them and yourself—for your shared imperfections?
- Is there something you want to say to this person that you've never had the words or space to express until now?
- How can you begin healing that relationship today, even if it's only within your heart?

Don't Tell Me to Be Grateful

for the Warrior who gave too much, too quietly, for too long

Dear Fellow Warrior,
Sometimes healing begins not in light, but in fire.
Let yourself rage.
Let yourself ruin the polite silence you were told to keep.
This is not bitterness.
This is acknowledgment.
And that's holy, too.

I am the storm I swallowed
so you could feel safe around me.
But today, I spit thunder.
Don't tell me to be grateful.
Grateful for what—
the hours I spent
learning how to smile through hell?
The decade I lost
dreaming of the life I should be living by now?

I should be somewhere else.
Don't you understand?
I was someone else—
Before the diagnosis rearranged my destiny,
before my name was written in hospital ink
instead of bold headlines and business plans.

I've watched people pass me,
building the life I dreamed of,
while I counted pills
and called that progress.
While I stitched strength from silence.

You think I'm resilient—
But I'm mad.
I'm livid.
I'm fire tucked beneath soft eyes.
I'm fury in a floral dress.
I'm what happens
when hope gets tired of being polite.

This isn't a phoenix story.
Not yet.
This is the burn.
The scream. The wreckage.
The *Why me?* screamed
so loud the universe should shake.

I want back the time I lost.
I want an apology from fate.
From my body.
From every doctor who said *"you're lucky"*
while I buried version after version of myself.

I am not okay.
And finally, I don't need to be.

Because this?
This rage— is the first honest thing
I've felt in a long time.

And maybe, just maybe,
this fire is not the end of me—
but the beginning
of something no longer willing
to shrink for someone else's comfort.

~

Reflection Prompt: *When Gratitude Isn't Enough*

- Have you ever felt pressured to hide your anger behind forced gratitude?

- What parts of your story have been misunderstood as strength when they were actually survival?
- What does it look like to honor your pain without apology?
- What truths have you been too polite to say out loud—and how could releasing them set you free?

The Beauty in My Scars

for those who trace their strength in the mirror

Dear Fellow Warrior,
This poem is a mirror.
Not the kind that hides what's been altered—
but the kind that celebrates it.
You are still beautiful.
Not despite the scars,
but because of them.

The sun slips through the blinds
like a lover who knows my secrets—
warm, soft, deliberate.
It kisses the corner of my lip,
crawls down the curve of my collarbone,
and meets the place where I always start my mornings:

those three soft ridges
etched just beneath my neck.

My fingers go there
without permission.
Every morning. Every time.
Like a ritual, like prayer, like proof.

They used to burn.
Now they hum.
Sometimes I press cocoa butter on them
like lipstick on old letters.
Sometimes I whisper apologies to the girl
I used to be— the one before the incisions,
before the drip of chemo,
before strength became a job
I never applied for.

But today,
I drag my fingers slow.
I trace them like poetry.
I wear them like lace.

These aren't flaws.
These are flames
that didn't consume me.

These are battle scars—
not blemishes. Not mistakes.
Art.

You want to know what happened?
You want to lean in and ask

what those raised lines mean,
as if your curiosity is more important
than my survival?

I'll tell you.
This is what resilience looks like.
This is the part of me
that doesn't shrink, doesn't fade,
doesn't need your permission
to be beautiful.

Yes— I wore long sleeves in the summer.
I've dodged mirrors, and side-eyes
and questions dipped in pity.

But I've also stood naked, alone,
beneath moonlight,
and found every scar
soft, sacred, mine.

I've counted my wounds
and still showed up to the next round.
I've swallowed nausea like clockwork
and still spoke life into my future.
I've cried between chemo chairs
and still dared to dream.

There's nothing pitiful
about this kind of power.
Nothing broken about this kind of beauty.

These scars?
They are my story.

My ceremony.
My sensuality.

I no longer beg them to fade.
I let them glisten.
I let them speak.
I let them seduce the shame right off my skin.

Because this is not the end of me.
This is where I began again— sultry, strong,
and still soft enough to believe in love.

If you've ever felt less-than
for what your skin has survived,
remember:
The world has no right to define your beauty
when you've redefined your life.

Wear your scars like silk.
Let them whisper your name.
And when you walk into a room—
do it like the storm you are.

~

Reflection Prompt: *The Story in Your Skin*

- What stories do your scars—visible or invisible—tell about your journey?
- How can you begin to honor them as symbols of strength rather than reminders of struggle?
- In what ways have you reclaimed your beauty on your own terms?

- What would it feel like to celebrate the body that carried you through your darkest seasons?
- How can you practice sensuality and softness as acts of power and self-love?

Becoming the Place: A Two-Part Return

for the one still waiting to be chosen, and the one who's learning to choose herself

Dear Fellow Warrior,
*Somewhere between childhood wonder and adult performance, we learned to tuck ourselves away to stay safe. But the child within you is still watching.
Still waiting. Still wondering if it's safe to come out.
And the place you've always searched for?
It isn't a room, a role, or a relationship.
It's the unfiltered you, stepping back into the light you were never meant to dim. This is your sacred return—
to the child you were, the woman you are,
and the home you're finally becoming.*

Part I: To the Child Still Waiting

For Little RiRi — and for the little one still inside you, too.

Dear little RiRi,
the girl with galaxies in her gaze
and thunder in her stride—
I see you now.
Not as a memory,
not as a photograph tucked between the pages,
but as the heartbeat behind every brave decision
I've ever made.

I'm sorry.
I didn't come sooner.
Didn't speak louder.
Didn't build you a fortress
before the world ever taught you fear.

You were just a girl
with scraped knees and sky-wide dreams,
believing that love would always be soft
and that smiles always meant safety.
You danced like your soul had never been interrupted.
You stood in your light so fully
it made the shadows nervous.

You were flourishing,
unfolding, becoming.

And then— the world came.
Not gently. Not asking.
It came like a storm without a name,
tracking mud through your sacred spaces,
replacing wonder with warnings,

teaching you shame
before I ever taught you grace.

And I— I let you shrink
so others could shine.
I dressed you in strength
without giving you time to rest.
I demanded you survive
when all you wanted was to be held.

But hear me now—
I am building a life that remembers you.
One that moves slower, laughs louder,
and makes space for softness.
I will never again trade your joy for approval.
You are not a phase I grew out of—
you are the truth I return to.

I promise: to carry your questions with care,
to honor your hope as holy,
to speak your name with tenderness
even when the world forgets how to be gentle.

We are no longer at odds. We are one.
You are not just the past—
you are the purpose.

If only you could see us now,
you'd witness the bloom from the seeds you planted—
the roots that clung to cracked earth,
now towering trees, defying the storms.
You'd see laughter where tears once fell,

and hands that once trembled with doubt
now building futures with steady grace.

You'd hear your name in whispered prayers
and joyful sighs,
a melody in the rhythm of our lives.
You'd know— your love never left.
It simply changed form.
And became us.

Because the deep-seeded roots
were able to stand the test of time,
weathering storms that bent branches
but never broke the will to grow.
They drank from the smallest streams of hope,
became stronger with every struggle,
and now— they hold steady beneath us,
silent but unwavering,
carrying the weight of our becoming.
Proof that we were always destined to rise.

And to the ones reading this:
Yes, you too have a child still waiting.
Still watching.
Still wondering when you'll return.

Whether you've held a baby in your arms or not,
you have a child to raise—
and that child is *you.*
The you before the world rewrote your script.
Before the silence. Before the shame.
Before you learned to trade softness for strategy.

You are raising that child
with every boundary you draw,
every no you finally say,
every time you choose rest over guilt,
joy over performance,
healing over hiding.

So protect them.
Speak to them.
Honor them.
Let them dream again.
Let them be loud again.
Let them be free.

~

Part II: Somewhere to Belong

I've spent my life on the edges—
palms pressed against glass,
watching rooms fill
with laughter I could never quite echo.

Tried on masks like outfits,
mirrored moods I didn't feel,
hoping someone would call it love,
or at least call it enough.

There were playgrounds where
my name got lost in translation,
lunch tables that felt like
auditions for worth.

I smiled anyway.
Played the part.
Folded my voice
into something softer,
something safer.

Even in rooms filled with people,
I learned how to disappear—
became a master of blending,
a quiet storm in a crowd too loud to notice
the weather in my eyes.

I searched for the right friend group,
the right shoes,
the right shade of silence
that wouldn't make them leave.

Never realizing
I was searching for home
in people who hadn't built one
for themselves.

I never felt Black enough
because I spoke with precision,
because I was respectful,
because my mother raised me with grace.

But I never felt white enough either—
my skin too bold,
my curves too loud,
my truth too different.

Always somewhere in between,
belonging to everyone and no one.
A borrowed seat at every table.
A guest in my own story.

I've shape-shifted to fit vibes
I thought I needed—
straightened my voice,
curved my edges,
lowered my light
to match the dim of the room.

Only to find,
I was the vibe.
I was the tone.
I was enough all along.

Some nights I prayed
to be picked,
to be seen without squinting.
Other nights I danced alone
in my bedroom mirror,
holding myself
like the apology I never got.

I became the in-between girl—
too much soul for small talk,
too much depth for shallow spaces.
And still, I watered gardens
that never grew me.

But maybe belonging
was never theirs to give.

Maybe it's what I create
each time I stop shrinking
and start standing,
each time I speak
and my voice doesn't flinch.

Maybe the place I've been looking for
isn't a crowd—
it's a mirror that doesn't distort,
a space that holds me without conditions.

Maybe I am the place.
And I am still becoming it.

~

Reflection Prompt: *Becoming the Place*

- What parts of yourself did you learn to hide just to survive?
- When did you begin shrinking to fit someone else's comfort?
- What would it look like to live, speak, and move as if you already belong?
- Write a letter that begins: *"I see you now..."* and let your inner child and your current self speak truth to each other.

IV. The Emergence

The Wings Unfold — When the Light Gets In
This is the part where the becoming begins — bold, soft,
and true.

This is when becoming
feels less like effort
and more like breath.
Your body remembers the breaking—
but your spirit has started to rise.

You didn't soar right away.
First, you cracked.
Then you wept.
Then you waited.
But when the light finally found its way in,
you opened.

Not because the pain was gone,
but because you learned to live beside it.
To laugh anyway. To rise anyway.
To feel again— fully, fiercely, without apology.

The shell didn't shatter into ruin—
it opened into a doorway.
Your wings, still trembling,
stretched toward destiny.
You were no longer just surviving—
you were arriving.

This is *the emergence:*
a quiet reclaiming of softness.
A bold return to joy.
Not the joy that performs—
but the kind that sustains.

And you didn't do it alone.
Hands caught you when you fell.
Voices whispered your name
when you forgot it.
Love, in its quietest form,
kept the light on.

The roots you once tried to outrun?
They weren't holding you back—
they were anchoring you here.

Now, you move with memory and momentum.
With peace that asks for no permission.
With purpose humming beneath your skin
like a song you've always known.

The wings didn't appear all at once— but they came.
They grew in silence, in truth,
with each boundary drawn,
each laugh released,
each *"yes"* that set you free.

And when you looked around—
at the water, the trees,
your own steady body—
you knew:

This is becoming.
Not escape.
Not arrival.
But presence.
Power.
Peace.

You are not who you were.
And thank God. You are becoming—
again and again.
And the world is brighter
because of it.

City of Champions

for the city that made me—brick, grit, and bold blood

Dear Fellow Warrior,
Where we come from shapes us.
This poem is a celebration of grit,
of pride, of neighborhoods that raised us
in resilience and rhythm.
It's a tribute to the fire we carry forward.

    Came up where the pavement talks,
    where fists get raised before they knock.
    Where hearts stay armored, pride runs deep,
    and dreams don't come unless you lose sleep.

    From the city with a granite face,
    where pride moves bold and moves with grace.
    Brockton—brick and backbone tough,
    we learned young that soft ain't enough.

    The glove? That's fight. The fist? That's Black.
    Power they tried to hold back.
    Boxer blood in every stride,
    lessons carved we wear with pride.

    This city don't hand out wins for free—
    it chisels your soul, then sets it free.

    We come from everywhere—
    Cape Verde to Haiti,

Dominican roots, Ghanaian blood,
Jamaican grit, and Brazilian love.

Melting pot of pride and power,
different tongues, same grind every hour.
Barbershop beats to church choirs' song,
a hundred flags, and they all belong.

You feel the rhythm in our streets—
unity rising where cultures meet.
Stay humble, hustle hard—it's law,
not just words, it's what I saw.

Led my squad on that hardwood floor,
Division 1—left it all, then gave more.
Victory wasn't just in the score,
it was proving we were built for more.

Now I lead where I once stood small—
in my city, answering the call.
From team captain to community voice,
this path ain't luck—it's a chosen choice.

Don't get it twisted—
this is legacy, this is fight.
This is Brockton—
built from pressure, burning bright.
Every stitch, every line,
carries the weight of where I'm from.

This ain't just design—
this is the heartbeat of the slums.
This is the grind behind the gloss,

the beauty born from every loss.

So when you see it, know it's true—
Brockton's spirit stitched right through.

~

Reflection Prompt: *Rooted in the Hustle*

- Think about the place or community that raised you.
- What lessons did it teach you about strength, pride, and perseverance?
- How has your environment shaped your identity and your fight?
- In what ways do you carry your hometown's spirit forward?
- What does it mean to you to represent where you're from with intention?

Greatest Influence

for the Warrior who turned fear into fuel

Dear Fellow Warrior,
Sometimes the very thing that tried to break you becomes the reason you rise.
This poem is a testament to that turning point—

where pain meets purpose
and survival becomes strength.

Who is my greatest influence?
Or rather, *what?*
The question may seem simple—
but the answer is complex.

I think my greatest influence is
the fear of failure.
A double-edged sword many can relate to.

My greatest influence is
the absence of my self-esteem in the past—
the confidence I lacked.
Striving for greatness
in an attempt to prove myself to me.

Rising above the self-hate,
embracing the beauty I once betrayed,
inspires me to try and achieve perfection.

An unachievable type of perfection.
Chasing reflections that will never hold still.
Fighting to outgrow the shadows I once lived in.

Fueling my fire with the doubt I left behind.

So now I rise, not to escape who I was—
but to honor who I've become.

What once held me back now pushes me forward.
Fear no longer owns me.

It shaped me, yes—
but I've learned to shape it, too.

And in that,
I've already won.

~

Reflection Prompt: *Shaping the Shadows*

- What fears have shaped you—and how have you learned to shape them in return?
- Are there parts of your past that still push you forward today?
- What would it look like to honor your progress without demanding perfection?
- How can you use the echoes of old doubts as fuel for your current power?

Between Tides and Triumphs

for the ones who've kept rising, even when no one saw them fall

---

Dear Fellow Warrior,
You've kept rising, even when no one saw you fall.
This poem honors the quiet victories—
the ones no one applauds, but that saved your life anyway.

I keep small notes—
moments when my spirit
stood confident, grateful, bright—
tiny sparks within the dark,
proof that life still breathes
amid the storms.

Each chapter turns like tides,
folding open fresh and new—
a chance to shed old skin,
to cleanse away the weight,
to heal, to rise, to honor
how far I've come.

I reach back to the child I was,
whispering softly— *"Remember your worth,
remember the fire
that carried you here."*

My life is not changed—
only the lens has shifted.
A lifetime chasing wins—
exams, designs, victories—
cancer, the mountain climbed in
chemotherapies and radiation.

Halfway there, eyes fixed
beyond the horizon,
moving steady through the storm,
learning strength
in perspective's tide.

I have learned to hold my power—
to be unapologetically me.
I will not auction my light
to those who fail to see its glow.

My time, my love, my energy—
too precious for shadows.
If they cannot meet me
where my worth lives,
I walk away—
bearing my fire,
with all its worth and tax.

~

Reflection Prompt: *Between Tides and Triumphs*

- What small moments of courage or gratitude have helped you keep going in your darkest times?
- How has your view of yourself changed through your journey?
- Reflect on the ways you protect your light and choose where to invest your energy.

Love Language

for the ones who speak soul before sound

Dear Fellow Warrior,
Not all love looks the same.
This is for the ones who love in unspoken ways—
through presence, through patience, through holding
space when words fall short.
This poem is a reminder that you are seen, even in
silence.

        Impressions of you stay stagnant
           in the crevasses of my mind.
Making me fall in love with the English language
          as if it were my first time—
             Hearing them.
             Hearing you.
         Makes me believe in love again.

      You sure know how to stimulate my time.
Craving someone's thoughts this badly must be a crime.
    I— dream of what it would be like to feel you.
          But not feel you feel you…
            You feel me?

        Feel you in the spiritual sense.
Way deeper than you ever thought you'd be able to go.
            Poetically,
        Sinking your soul into mine,
    drowning in the sea of passionate abyss.
         So deep, but not lost.
         So lost, but still found.
           So beautiful,
       I always want you around.

Where's your crown?
Because every time you speak,
I swear it's scripture.
Each syllable is a sermon I wasn't ready for,
but needed.
You got me baptized in your rhythm,
tongue-tied in testimony,
and I've never been more willing
to drown in divinity.

See—
this ain't just love, it's language.
A dialect only we seem to understand.
When your eyes meet mine,
the silence translates into poems
I haven't even written yet.

You are the metaphor
I didn't know I was searching for—
a stanza I reread in every stranger
but only ever recognized in you.

Your presence feels like déjà vu,
like I met you in another lifetime,
maybe we were galaxies
orbiting the same sun,
or verses in the same sacred text,
whispered into being
before time began.

How do you do that?
Make me question gravity,

and time, and self
all in a single glance?

So I ask again— *Where's your crown?*
Because your soul sits heavy like royalty,
and I'd kneel just to understand
the way you think.

You're the spark behind my stanzas,
the muse I never knew I was worthy of.
And when you look at me,
I feel like art.
Not just seen—understood.
Not just loved—chosen.

With you, every moment becomes a metaphor.
Every breath, a blessing.
Every glance, a gospel.

You awaken the parts of me
that only poetry could reach.
You remind me that I'm not hard to love,
just waiting for someone fluent in my language.

And baby, you speak me fluently.
You mirror my magic back to me
with a smile that feels like sunrise,
and a presence that hushes
every storm inside me.

So I'll ask just one last time— *Where's your crown?*
Because when I'm with you,

heaven feels close.
And I swear—you make royalty look easy.

Because this love isn't loud or performative—
it's fluent.
It speaks to the woman I've become,
not just the girl I was.
It doesn't try to fix me— it feels me.
It's not a rescue— it's a reflection.
A reminder:
that real love doesn't demand you dim—
it honors your shine.

And in your arms,
I didn't lose myself.
I found a language
that sounded like home
in my own voice.

~

Reflection Prompt: *Fluent Love*

- When have you felt deeply understood—beyond words?
- What does it mean for someone to *"speak your language"?*
- How has your idea of love evolved as you've grown into yourself?
- Are you fluent in your own emotional needs—and are you allowing someone in who honors them?

A New Kind of Legacy Being Built

for the generation choosing to heal forward

Dear Fellow Warrior,
We don't inherit only names and heirlooms—we inherit pain, patterns, silence.
But what we choose to pass on? That's power.
This poem is for the ones rewriting the script.
The cycle-breakers. The brave.
*The legacy is shifting—because of **you**.*

    We didn't choose the wounds,
    but we chose not to keep bleeding.

    We come from lines
    where silence was survival,
    and love was often
    measured by labor,
    not laughter.

    Where softness was swallowed
    so the next mouth could eat.
    Where apologies died in throats
    before they ever reached daylight.

    But we—
    we are something different.

We feel on purpose.
We name what hurt.
We say, *"This ends with me,"*
even when our voices shake.

We are the first to go to therapy.
The first to say *"I love you"*
without needing a reason.
The first to set a boundary
and not flinch.
To rest, without guilt.
To rise, without shame.

We are asking questions
no one dared ask before.
We are parenting ourselves
while parenting others.
We are forgiving,
without forgetting.

This is not rebellion— it's repair.
This is not disrespect— it's redirection.

We honor what they survived.
But we refuse to pass on
what nearly broke them.
We hold the weight,
not because we must—
but because we are strong enough
to put it down.

And in doing so,
we build something new—

out of grace, out of courage,
out of fire and softness and *truth*.

We are not just healing.
We are building
a new kind of legacy—
where love feels safe,
and freedom feels familiar.
Where the next generation
doesn't have to choose
between being whole
and being loved.

We are the turning point.
The rupture and the rebuild.
The ancestors' dream,
becoming real.

~

Reflection Prompt: *A Legacy Rewritten*

- What inherited patterns, beliefs, or expectations are you choosing to release?
- How does your healing serve not just you, but those who came before—and those who will come after?
- What does a *"new kind of legacy"* look like in your family, your community, or your own becoming?

The Weight of a Thought

for the one learning to prune their own mind garden

Dear Fellow Warrior,
Your mind is your fiercest battlefield—
and your greatest sanctuary.
This piece is for the days when your thoughts feel louder than truth, and your fears try to disguise themselves as facts.
You are not what anxiety says.
You are not your lowest moment.
You are the master of your mind—
and you get to choose what grows there.

Some days,
it starts as a whisper—
a thought too small to name
but heavy enough to bend my spine.

You'll never catch up.
You're falling behind.
You're too much.
You're not enough.

And suddenly,
my breath feels borrowed.
My joy—on layaway.
My hope—backordered.

No one told me
how much power a single thought could hold.
How fast it could spiral
into self-doubt, into stillness,
into stories that never belonged to me.

I've walked through hallways in my mind
lined with mirrors that distort.
Reflections that lie.
Echoes that shame.
Rooms labeled
"Not good enough"
"Try harder"
"Almost."

But I'm learning—
I am the landlord of this mind.
I get to evict what no longer serves me.

So now,
I talk back.
I replace *"What if I fail?"*
with *"But what if I fly?"*
I ask myself
if I would say these things
to the child I once was.

And when the answer is no—
I rewrite.
I reframe.
I return.
To kindness.

To clarity.
To compassion that doesn't require a performance.

I tend to my thoughts like a garden—
pulling weeds of shame,
watering seeds of truth,
and resting in the shade
of what I now know:

A thought is not a prophecy.
A mood is not a map.
And fear— fear is just the body's way
of asking for gentleness.

So I give it.
To myself.
To my mind.
To my future.

Because healing isn't just in the body.
It's in the thoughts
you choose to believe.

~

Reflection Prompt: *The Garden Within*

- What thought patterns have held you back from peace, joy, or self-worth?
- How can you begin replacing those thoughts with truth and compassion?
- What would it look like to speak to yourself the way you would to someone you love?

- What kind of garden are you growing in your mind—and what does it need right now to flourish?

Walk a Mile (Don't Let Me Be Another Ghost)

for the Warrior who's tired of being admired but not understood

---

Dear Fellow Warrior,
They see your power but miss your pain.
They call you strong but never stop to ask what it costs.
This poem is a challenge, a prayer, and a plea:
Walk with us.
Not to judge, fix, or applaud— but to witness.
We are more than what we've survived.
We are here, waiting to be seen beyond the armor.

I dare you to walk a mile in my shoes.
Bet you won't make it past the first block.
These soles are worn from running on empty,
from pacing through problems no one talks about.

Pressure sits on my back like a second spine—
heavy, silent,
but still I rise every damn time.

I've walked through rooms full of voices,
but none of them ever called my name right.
They laughed at the wrong pitch,
asked the wrong questions,
left when it mattered most.

Everybody wants the crown,
but no one wants the bruises.
No one sees the nights I cried on carpet floors,
praying like God was the only one listening—
because He was.

I carry expectations like they come with my bloodline.
First to go, first to grow,
first to feel the cold from the ones who stayed behind.

Success turns people strange.
Suddenly, I'm the villain
for refusing to shrink.

I don't wear armor—
I am the armor.
Built from betrayal and bounced checks,
from closed doors and *"maybe next time"* texts.

But I've also been a quiet war for as long as I can remember—
smiling while bleeding,
dancing while drowning,
living while feeling nothing at all.

You say you love me.
But do you see me?

The shadows I carry?
The girl who learned too young
how to comfort herself because no one else would?

I don't want to wear masks anymore.
I'm tired of performing the version of me
that makes people feel comfortable.

I need someone who doesn't flinch at the truth,
someone who stays
when I stop pretending.

Resilience ain't a cute quote.
It's waking up when you don't want to.
Fighting battles no one claps for.
Smiling with cracked lips
and hands still working.

Please— don't become just another name
on my list of people who meant well
but never really listened.

Don't love the idea of me
and miss the soul standing right in front of you.
Don't hear my strength
and ignore my ache.
Don't see the wins
and miss the losses I bled for.

This ache is older than you,
but you— you still have the chance to be different.

So listen.
Not to my words,
but to the silence behind them.
That's where I live.
That's where I'm waiting—
to finally be known.

So yeah—
I dare you to walk a mile in my shoes.
Not to see what it's like,
but to feel what it takes to survive
and still dream
while begging— just once—
to be truly seen.

~

Reflection Prompt: *Ghosted in the Light*

- When have you been praised for your strength while feeling deeply unseen?
- What version of you shows up to be accepted—and what part of you waits in the shadows?
- How can you begin to honor the full truth of your story without shrinking, masking, or softening your voice for others' comfort?
- Write a poem or journal entry that begins with the line: *"You say you love me, but do you see me?"*

Why Black Joy?

for those who wonder why we name ourselves

Dear Fellow Warrior,
Because joy is resistance.
Because despite what's been taken,
we still laugh, dance, love, and shine.
This poem is a celebration of that unbreakable spirit—
our right to live loudly.

Some ask,
why must it be Black Joy?
Why carve out months, movements, menus,
for what should belong to everyone?

It's a fair question—
if you've never had to ask
where your reflection went
in history books,
on movie screens,
in boardrooms,
or in menus
where the soul of our seasonings
was served without our names.

You see,
when you are the default,
you don't have to declare it.
You don't have to say
"White-owned business,"

or *"White Lives Matter,"*
because the world has already
whispered it to you
in the silence of systems
built in your image.

But for us,
nothing was given.
We had to claim it.
Name it. Shout it—
to hear our own echo
bounce back in a world
that tried to hush us.

Black Joy is not a division.
It's a declaration
that we are still here.
Still whole.
Still worthy of celebration.

Black History Month
is not a bonus track—
it's the verses cut from the album
you've heard all your life.
We add it back in
so the song makes sense.

When we say *Black Lives Matter,*
we're not excluding.
We are insisting— on visibility
in places where we are too often
left unseen until it is too late.

And when we say *Black-owned,*
we are not closing the door.
We are opening it
to a lineage of labor,
invention, and perseverance
that has often been
uncredited,
undervalued,
unpaid.

This is not a rejection
of anyone else's worth.
It is a long-overdue celebration
of our own.

So when you see us naming ourselves—
in our joy, in our grief,
in our food, in our freedom—
know this:
We are not asking for more.
We are claiming what's always been ours.

Pull up a chair,
and taste the history.
It's seasoned with love, resistance,
and a future where everyone eats
and no one forgets who grew the garden.

~

Reflection Prompt: *Joy as Resistance*

- How do you claim and celebrate your joy amid the weight of history and struggle?
- What does Black Joy—or your own version of joyful self-affirmation—mean to you?
- In what ways is your joy an act of resistance, remembrance, or restoration?
- How can embracing joy strengthen your journey forward—and create space for others to do the same?

V. The Ascension

The Wings — Reborn in Truth, Carried by Grace
You've earned your wings. Now, you rise.

This isn't just flight—
it's a return to your truest self.
You moved through fire,
sat still in the cocoon,
wept beside the unraveling,
and stayed when it would've been easier to disappear.

You didn't just survive.
You softened. You sharpened.
You surrendered. You soared.

Now, *you rise*—not only for yourself,
but for every version of you who prayed for this
moment, and for the ones still learning how to believe
again.

Ascension isn't perfection. It's presence.
It's power reclaimed in full.
It's speaking from the scar, not the wound.
It's refusing to shrink.
It's leading with love without losing yourself.

You no longer wait for permission.
You no longer perform to be seen.
This is your homecoming:

to your voice, your calling,
your freedom.

You carry the ones who lifted you,
the roots that grounded you,
the wings that grew slowly but surely.

This is your revolution.
Your joy is generational.
Your healing is a ripple effect.

You are not becoming anymore.
You are.

And the world is brighter because you didn't stay hidden.

Welcome to the sky you built.

Welcome to *The Ascension.*

From Soil to Sunlight

for the ones growing in silence, still reaching for the light

---

Dear Fellow Warrior,
Growth isn't glamorous.
It's messy. Tender.
Rooted in shadow before it ever touches light.
This poem is a reminder
that even buried things can bloom.
Especially you.

If only you could see us now—
you'd witness the seeds you planted,
roots wrapped in quiet defiance,
deep enough to hold the weight
of everything we became.

We weathered it all:
the doubts, the droughts,
the moments that nearly cracked us open.
Still, we rose.
Still, we reached.

Beneath us, the roots held steady—
unseen but sacred,
a living testimony
that the becoming never stopped,
even when the world did.

A strong soul is like a wild sunflower—
rooted in rocky soil,
yet still rising to meet the sun.
Golden petals edged with grit,
wind-whipped but unwavering.
They bow when they need to,
but they never forget how to stand.

And when the storm passes,
they shine—not in spite of the rain,
but *because of it.*
Every droplet,
a reminder they're still here.

Their roots run deep—
into legacy, into lineage,
into something older than pain
and wider than fear.
They grow in silence.
They rise without applause.
They become beauty
even when no one's watching.

You are that bloom—
born of struggle,
bathed in shadow,
breaking through
toward your own kind of light.

And baby—
you're unstoppable now.

~

Reflection Prompt: *Rooted and Rising*

- Reflect on a time when you faced hardship but kept going—even if no one else saw it.
- What inner strength or truth revealed itself through your struggle?
- What roots—your values, your ancestors, your faith—have helped anchor you during storms?
- What does it mean for you to keep growing, even when no one's clapping yet?
- How do you honor your growth when the world still expects you to bloom quietly?

Ode to the Bison in Me

for the Warrior whose detour became her destiny

Dear Fellow Warrior,
This poem is a tribute to the fierce, unbreakable spirit within you— the bison that carries you through storms and detours.
It's a testament to how pain and hardship can become the very fuel for purpose and growth.
Let it remind you that your survival is a powerful roar, a legacy in motion, and a call to rise beyond what tries to break you.

I didn't know the road would curve like this—
that cancer would become my compass,
that pain would push me into purpose,
that the fire meant to stop me
would forge me instead.

Fifteen and free—just a girl with a gift,
a needle, some fabric, and faith stitched in.
I was just doing what I loved—
didn't dream it would turn to checks.

It was never for the money.
It was always for the making.

And then came the days when my body broke—
chemo cocktails, radiation rhythms,
doctor visits punched into every week.

No office job could wait for me,
so I worked for myself.
Ran my business between treatments,
built something beautiful from survival.

Howard University was a whisper on my vision board,
a dream too bold to speak aloud—
but I did.
And it listened.

It opened its arms
and called me Bison.

I stepped on campus, not just with books,
but with battle scars and business plans.

The spirit of the Yard wrapped me in warmth—
my skin, my story, finally in sync.

This was more than a school.
It was a *homecoming*
to a part of me I didn't know I missed.

I could have taken the fast track—
the same school, the easy loop,
the path that looked safe
before my cells betrayed me.

But God had a detour.
One that led me to Howard's gates,
to legacies, to laughter, to love.

My grandmother's steps echoed in mine,
her dreams, now degrees,
her pride pressed into every page I turned.

I knew she was watching.
I knew she was beaming.

And now—MBA in hand,
battle-won, purpose-wrapped,
entrepreneur still standing, still growing—

I say **thank you**
to the thing that tried to break me.
Cancer, you rerouted me.
You stopped me from chasing what was safe
and started me on what was sacred.

I didn't just survive. *I soared.*

I became a Howard Bison.
And I will never forget
the roar it took to rise.

Special Dedication:
To my Howard University School of Business cohort—
You were more than classmates.
You were lifelines.
In study sessions and silent battles,
in hallway hugs and post-presentation praise,
you reminded me I belonged in every room I entered.
You saw the grind behind my grace
and celebrated the woman behind the wins.
You held space for my becoming—
not just as a scholar,
but as a whole healing human.
For that, I thank you.
H.U.
You know.

~

Reflection Prompt: *The Sacred Detour*

- What unexpected detours in your life have shaped the person you are today?
- How have your struggles led to new purpose, strength, or identity?
- In what ways has pain turned into power for you?

- Who are the ancestors, mentors, or inner voices that walked with you through the fire?
- What would it look like to thank your past—even the hard parts—for helping you find your roar?

Rude Gyal

for every woman who stopped asking for permission to shine

Dear Fellow Warrior,
This one is for the sacred callings that won't let you go.
The dreams that chase you back.
This poem is about purpose—
persistent, divine, and undeniably yours.
It'll find you. Patience is key.

Yuh know seh mi a rude gyal—
di baddest of dem all.
The way mi swing mi hips,
mi mek dem pause, mi mek dem fall.
Mi step in sweet like sugarcane,
but mi fierce like pepper too.
Mi body speak in rhythms
dat yuh soul cyaan undo.

Mi skin glow like golden honey,
mi hair wild like Island breeze,
mi nuh beg no man fi nothin',
mi move how mi please.
Mi love di curve, mi love di shape,
mi confidence too loud to fake.
Mi strut like runway royalty—
dem cyaan keep up, so dem hate.

Every step mi tek is freedom,
every glance a silent claim.
Mi nah compete, mi complete,
mi play mi own damn game.
Mi lips talk fire,
mi eyes write verse,
mi walk in purpose—
never curse.

Mi crown never slip,
not even on bad days.
Mi rise up strong,
mi blaze new ways.
Dem cyaan dim mi light,
mi was born for da throne.
Mi rule dis life—
solid, fierce, full grown.

Mi nuh shrink fi no one,
mi nah play small.
Mi tek up space,
mi tek it all.
So if yuh cyaan handle di glow,

kindly move aside—
mi nah dull fi comfort,
mi nah run fi hide.

~

And now I know—
I was never too much.
I was never too loud.
I was never too bold.
I was just waiting to believe
what I always carried.

From this day forward,
I don't chase validation—
I embody the truth.
I don't question my power—
I wear it like skin.

I'll never dim my light again.
Because confidence?
It's not something I perform.
It's who I am.
And I'll never lack it again.

~

Reflection Prompt: *Unapologetic Power*

- When was the last time you truly embraced your power without apology?
- What parts of your identity—your culture, your style, your voice—deserve more celebration?

- How can you walk through the world more boldly, rooted in your worth and your fire?
- If you wore your confidence like a crown, what would shift in how you show up?

Legacy in Motion / Harsh Realities

for the Warrior who made it—and still had to fight to stay whole

---

Dear Fellow Warrior,
Success doesn't silence the ache.
This poem is for the ones who made it—
and still feel the weight.
For those who've achieved everything they dreamed of,
only to discover that rising comes with its own reckoning.
You're not ungrateful.
You're evolving.
This is your celebration and your truth.
You're allowed to hold both.

Part I: Legacy in Motion

I beat the odds.
Twice.

Once against cancer,
and again against every barrier
that tried to tell me who I could not be.

I became exactly what I dreamed of:
a fashion designer, a writer, a visionary, an activist—
a survivor with a story stitched in truth.

I was honored as **Alumni of the Year** by Brockton High
School— recognized not just for my success,
but for how I showed up for my community since I was
a student in the Brockton Public School systems.
A product of grind, grit, and giving back,
I carried that same spirit into everything that followed.

I earned my first degree in **Fashion Design and
Production** from **Lasell College**—
where I wasn't just a student; I was a standout.
Recognized for more than talent— but for character,
contribution, and community.

The faculty saw something in me
and honored it.
I was awarded the prestigious **Book Award**,
named top of my class—
not just by grade, but by grace.

They didn't know I was sick.
But they chose me.
The professors.
The professionals.
Not just as a student—
but as a leader in the making.

And while at Lasell,
I was chosen to attend the **London College of Fashion**—
one of the most respected fashion institutions in the world.
Even then, they saw my light.
My gifts were undeniable.

After beating cancer I took my purpose further—
earning my **MBA from the illustrious Howard University**, the Mecca.
Where I didn't just study business—
I built it.
While working at the **Center for Career Excellence**,
I helped guide the next generation—
within and beyond the classroom.
Mentoring students as I mentored myself,
through healing I didn't always speak of.

Even in the silence, I showed up.
And the community saw me.
They honored me.

And I kept going.

I became the **first Black writer** at *The Martha's Vineyard Times*
to create and launch my own editorial brand:
Voices bySharisse—
a home for the unheard.
A celebration of Islanders of color—
documented, dignified, and deeply seen.

My fashion brand went international.
I won awards.
Dressed bodies and minds.
Mentored through advocacy.
Spoke truth into systems that once ignored us.

I became the woman I once needed.
And still—some days,
I carry it all alone.

Because while my light has always been seen,
while my gifts have always been recognized,
the woman *behind* the success?
She's still learning to be held.
Still learning that survival was never the whole story—
becoming is.

~

Part II: Harsh Realities

Rolling over to the warm sun
kissing my face each morning—
greeted by the sound of unnecessary landscaping,
keeping my cushy Buckhead apartment pristine.

The weight of guilt drags me out of bed
as I set out to achieve my dreams—
dreams that moved me from Massachusetts
all the way down to the big ATL.

Leaving a trail of tears,
because loved ones could never understand
that this move had nothing to do with them.

No one ever told me that being the first generation
to leave home to pursue higher education
would bring more isolation
than celebration.

But loneliness hit like a desert storm
before I even left home.
Staying in a city where your dreams can't fit
wasn't an alternative I was willing to live with.

No one warned me about the resentment
running through the veins of the people I love most—
Certain family and friends who never brag or boast,
but out of sight, out of mind, *right?*—
I might as well be a ghost.

Daring to stand out
makes you practically unseen
when haters pray for your downfall
behind doors that are squeaky clean.

If someone told me
that once I left,
I'd never be able to return again,
maybe I would've stayed.
Maybe I would've folded.
But when I close my eyes
and imagine that life—
I wake up in screams.

I was 15 when I started building legacy.
Launched businesses
while other kids were still learning how to dream.
All I ever wanted was community—
like-minded people,
souls who saw the vision.
But I've met more who hoped I'd fail
than ones who prayed I'd rise.
More eyes watching for my fall
than hands reaching to lift me.

That's why I never press snooze.
There's too much purpose in my pulse.
Too much to prove—
and even more to protect.

But no matter the path,
it's like loneliness is waiting at every turn.
What I thought would be comradery
was really just quiet competition.
Smile in your face—
then stab you in the back.

If you're striving for success,
you're already under attack.
But what's the alternative?
To stay small, complacent,
and pretend you're content?
Nah, fuck that.

I'd rather be patient.
I know my time will come.

They say it's lonely at the top for a reason—
and it ain't just for a season.
That shit is for life.

A contractual agreement
signed in pain and strife.
But that's the price you pay
when you're one of the chosen ones.
Just you— and the Holy One.

Jesus Christ...
Why is being supportive
such a rare trait in this journey of life?

They say the devil hears
the same prayers we send up to God—
so your faith must stay intact,
even when there's no applause.

Because when you lean into Him,
you bounce back.
You spring up.
You rise from the ashes.

You see— our success is inevitable.
Faith in ourselves? Inseparable.

Faith that if we keep moving forward,
we'll be rewarded in surplus.

So the battle continues.
Just keep
pursuing your purpose.

Reflection Prompt: *The Cost of Elevation*

- What milestones are you most proud of—and how did it feel to reach them without the support you expected?
- How has success shifted your sense of home or belonging?
- What would it look like to thrive in your purpose while still protecting your peace?
- Who are the people who truly celebrate you—and how can you make space for more of that energy?

THE FORMULA: A Poem of Gratitude for My People

written in honor of the ones who loved me into becoming

Part I: For My Sisters

You are not just blood—
you are backbone.
Not just friend—
you are frequency,
tuned to the ache in my silence
and the joy I didn't yet know how to name.

You were there in my becoming—
braiding love into my hair on the front steps,
clapping for me when I forgot to clap for myself.
You were the hush in the chaos,
the *"I got you"* when the world said *"You're too much."*

To the elders—
the aunties, the wise ones,
the women who walked ahead and turned back—
you covered me in prayer
before I even knew I needed it.
You taught me strength could wear lipstick,
and softness could hold storms.
You made safe space look like home.

To the ride-or-dies, the soul-keepers,
the ones who knew what I was feeling
before I found the words—
you stood guard when I was fragile,
laughed me back to light,
sat with me in the shadows.
You didn't ask me to be strong—
you reminded me I already was.

This is deeper than friendship.
This is divine design.
This is the beauty of a circle
where no one stands alone.
We don't compete. *We complete.*
We don't tear down. *We testify.*

To the sistahs in the struggle and the celebration—
you are rhythm and resistance,
you are Sunday praise and weekday power.
You are the ones who keep the culture
while carrying the world.

You made me feel safe just by being there—
a nod, a knowing, a glance across the room.
You didn't have to say a word—
and still, I knew I wasn't alone.

~

Part II: For My Brothers

You are not just presence—
you are protection.
Not just strength—
you are sanctuary.

I grew up under your watch—
big brothers, neighborhood guardians,
the ones who stood at the bus stop,
made sure I got home safe,
told the world without words:
"You don't mess with her. She's got people."

You've shielded me from storms
and walked with me through fire.
Even when life beat you down—
you stood up for me.
That's a love I'll never forget.

To the brothers who ask, *"You good?"*
and wait for the real answer—
you're the ones who show up
not just when it's easy,
but when it matters most.

To the brothers who cry and still lead,
who protect with purpose and love with depth—
you are kings,
even when the world forgets to crown you.

To the ones who hold space for each other,
who lift one another higher,
who remind us all:
healing is masculine too.

This is not just about loyalty—
it's about legacy.
It's about holding each other
through the breaking and the building.
It's about knowing someone has your back,
even when you're too tired to ask.

~

Epilogue: The Gratitude

You are the reason I knew I could grow.
You are the net that caught me when I jumped.
The mirror that showed me myself when I started to
forget.

You made my journey sacred—
not because it was easy,
but because I never had to walk it alone.

This is the formula:
Love without condition.
Support without ego.
Presence without pride.

Thank you for the nights you stayed,
the words you offered,
the silence you shared,
the armor you gave me
when I didn't know how to protect my own heart.

This is my love letter
to every sister, every brother,
every elder, every chosen one
who loved me into being.
I carry you with me everywhere I go.

You wrapped me in community
when I was most unraveled.
You prayed me through.
You fed my dreams and spoke my name in rooms
I hadn't even entered yet.
You saw me not as who I was—
but as who I could be.
You are my safe space.
You are a forever part of this healing.
Thank you for loving me
into my legacy.

Reflection Prompt: *The Ones Who Lifted You*

- Who are the people—by blood or by bond—who saw you when you couldn't see yourself? Write them a letter of thanks.
- Then write one to yourself—for surviving, for trusting, for becoming. Reflect on what it means to be held, and how you can offer that same grace to someone else.

This Smile Has a Story (But I'm Not Telling It Today)

for the ones who choose joy without needing to justify it

Dear Fellow Warrior,
You don't owe anyone your backstory to deserve your smile.
Joy doesn't always need a reason—sometimes, it's the reward.
So let today be light.
Let today be laughter.
Let today be yours.

There's something about today—
the way the breeze brushed my cheek

like it remembered my name.
The way my coffee hit just right,
and the sun made everything golden
like a filter I didn't have to earn.

No, I won't explain this smile.
Not today.

Not when the music in my head
is louder than my doubts.
Not when my hips are swaying
for no one but me,
and the sidewalk is my stage.

You see, I've carried heavy.
But today, I'm light.
And baby, I'm dancing.

I'm laughing at something
that wouldn't be funny in a courtroom—
but is hilarious when it's just me and the sky
and that one friend who gets it.

I'm glowing without needing a reason.
I'm flirting with the moment.
I'm choosing the sweetest treat.
I'm buying the flowers—*for myself.*

This smile?
It has survived things you'll never know.
But you don't have to know.
Not today.

Today is joy— loud, unbothered,
and soft as whipped cream
on a rooftop dessert
with my hair a mess
and my heart in bloom.

I'll tell you the story another time.
For now— just smile back.

~

Reflection Prompt: *The Joy You Don't Have to Explain*

- When was the last time you let yourself feel good without needing a reason?
- How would it feel to embrace joy simply because you deserve it?
- Write about a moment—recent or past—when your smile came from within.
No backstory. No disclaimers. Just joy.

Stitching My Soul

for the creator who turns fabric into freedom

Dear Fellow Warrior,
Needle. Thread. Breath.
This piece is about piecing yourself back together through the art you make and the love

you dare to give yourself again.
Fashion was never just fabric.
It was therapy.

A conversation between the heart and the head,
threads of thought tangled in a dance—
my heart beats with fire,
my head sharp with design,
together, they sew.

I am a creator,
a weaver of dreams,
taking nothing and breathing life into it—
a blank canvas of fabric and thread,
becoming something more,
something *one of a kind*.

I speak through stitches,
my gift is my voice,
my hands tell stories
that words cannot express.
A swirl of color, a bold line,
each piece is a reflection of my soul.
I design not just for the eye,
but for the *heart*.

I love this craft,
the artistry of passion—
every cut, every fold,
every pattern born from the depths of my being.
I am not just creating clothes,
I am giving life to something that didn't exist before.

I am forging a story,
a vision made real.

Sewing is my soulmate—
the rhythm of the needle,
the hum of the machine,
each stitch a love letter to creation.
With every pull, every loop,
we intertwine,
bound by a bond that is unspoken,
but understood in every thread I weave.

This is not just fashion;
it's my truth, my voice,
sewn into every thread,
every seam, every breath of design.

With every stitch,
I stitch my spirit into the fabric,
and the world will see me—
not just through the clothes,
but through the creativity
I wear on my sleeves.

~

Reflection Prompt: *Sewn from the Soul*

- What passion or craft in your life allows you to express your deepest self?
- How can you honor the story you are weaving, both for yourself and for the world to see?

- What does your creative process reveal about your healing, your history, or your power?

Like Home

for the one who never stopped searching for safe

Dear Fellow Warrior,
Home isn't always a place.
Sometimes it's a person,
a rhythm,
a memory that wraps around you like a second skin.
This poem is a return to that sanctuary—
the space where your soul can finally exhale,
where love feels like breath,
like water,
like the divine.
May it remind you:
You are worthy of a love that feels
like home.

My love is like,
forehead kisses leaving impressions on your mind,
running down your spine
because you know it's a symbol of my love
and you can feel just how much I mean it.

My love is like,
warm summer rain
tapping on the windowpane to say hello,
but you already ran outside to greet it.

My love is like,
a calming wave of summer air
when you need relief.

My love is like,
the lines from your go-to song,
the familiar chords of your favorite tune.

My love is like,
the warmth of a thousand blankets,
your favorite movies,
hot chocolate and marshmallows
keeping you warm on a cold winter night.

My love is like,
when the sun rises in the morning,
bursting through your curtains,
so bright you can feel it
without even opening your eyes.

My love is like,
your escape.
Your personal getaway.
Only you can see me—
even though I am in plain sight.

My love is like,
breathing again after nearly being swallowed.

Surfacing from the depths
just in the nick of time.

My love is like,
a blessing.

My love is like,
everything you see in your mother's eyes
when she tells you she loves you,
and you wholeheartedly accept her words—
embracing them without hesitation.

My love is like,
everything you thought you needed and more.
The answer to all your questions,
even if you walk into the unknown.

My love is like,
water to quench your thirst.

My love is like,
you can't savor it,
but it still feeds your soul.
Though scentless,
it fills your air with nostalgia.

My love is like,
what has yet to come—
the excitement of what is to be.

My love is like,
you didn't even realize what you were missing

until you found it.
But now you just can't seem to live without it.

My love is...
Unconditional.
Unforgettable.
Unbreakable.
Unshakable.
Indescribable.
Irreplaceable.
Iridescent.

My love is like,
God.
You can't see it,
but you know it's always there.
You can't hold it,
but you can always feel it.

My love is like,
a religion.
A remedy. The cure.

My love is like,
not going down without a fight.
The answer to your prayers,
what keeps you up at night.

My love is like
no one else's.

My love is like,
home.

And now—
I see it. I am it.
I've fallen in love with the woman I've become.
Not because she's perfect,
but because she chose to rise
when every reason told her to fold.

I look in the mirror and I know—
I am the magic.
I am the muse.
I am the sanctuary I was searching for.

I am proud of me.
Proud of my persistence.
Proud of the power I reclaimed in silence.
Proud of how I kept my softness
even while sharpening my strength.

I became the alchemist—
turning diagnosis into destiny,
loss into legacy,
pain into purpose.

I made poetry from pressure.
I made light out of loneliness.
I took every lemon life gave me
and made a whole orchard.
Lemonade,
lemon balm,
sunshine in a bottle.

The universe is smiling down at me
because I chose not just to survive—

I chose to bloom.
And baby,
I bloomed wild.
I bloomed free.
I bloomed into me.

~

Reflection Prompt: *Home as a Feeling*

- What does *"home"* feel like to you—not as a place, but as a presence?
- Who or what makes you feel deeply seen, safe, and whole?
- How can you cultivate that sense of safety and rootedness within yourself, regardless of your surroundings?
- What version of you are you finally falling in love with?

The Best Thing That Could Have Happened

for anyone who had to break before they bloomed

Dear Fellow Warrior,
What if the very thing that broke you was also the thing that rebuilt you—

stronger, softer, more sure of who you are?
This final piece is a reflection of gratitude
for the pain that made purpose possible,
for the diagnosis that rewrote my destiny,
and for every obstacle that opened a door I never knew I needed.

I would've never chosen it.
But I would've never changed it.
Not the diagnosis.
Not the silence.
Not the nights I cried so hard
my ribs remembered.

Because somewhere inside the wreckage,
I found the blueprint.
Not of who I was before,
but of who I had the chance to become.

Cancer came for my body
but gifted me my life.
It handed me truth I wasn't asking for—
but now I wouldn't trade.

And maybe your pain
didn't wear a hospital gown—
maybe it wore betrayal, or burnout,
or a kind of grief that walks in silence.
But still,
you rose.
Not despite the pain,
but because of it.

And if you listen closely,
you'll hear it—
the whisper that says,
"This was never the end.
This was the beginning
of everything real."

We thought we were doing great before…
but now— we are **truly unstoppable.**

Because somewhere between the silence and the suffering,
I found something even deeper than survival.
I found my **voice.**

The same voice that once went unheard—
even when my body was screaming for help.
The same voice that was silenced
until the tumor grew so large
I could barely speak at all.
But pain has a way of teaching you
what power really is.
And this journey?
It didn't just return my health—
it returned me to myself.

Now, I don't just speak.
I **own** my voice.
I write with it.
I lead with it.
I **heal** with it.

Because the most powerful thing I've ever done
was reclaim the parts of me
they once tried to ignore.

This is not just the best thing that could have happened.
This was the becoming.
This was the awakening.
This was the moment I realized—

I am the voice.
And I am no longer afraid to use it.

The Warrior Society Playlist

A sonic journey through survival, strength, and soul.

This is more than just a playlist—it's a sonic sanctuary. Handpicked for my Dear Fellow Warriors, *The Warrior Society Playlist* is a collection of 50+ powerful tracks that move through every mood: from grit to grace, from heartbreak to healing, from soul-stirring stillness to electric triumph.

You'll find ballads that hold you gently, anthems that remind you of your strength, and beats that demand you dance your way back to yourself. These songs were chosen with intention—for the quiet moments, the comeback moments, and everything in between.

Whatever stage of the journey you're in, there's a song here that speaks your language. Let this playlist hold you, hype you, heal you—and remind you that you are never alone.

These are just a few of the powerful songs that helped me through my own healing. May they carry you through yours. Listen as you heal, rise, reflect, and reclaim.

- "Ain't No Mountain High Enough" – Marvin Gaye & Tammi Terrell
- "As I Am" – H.E.R
- "Back on 74" – Jungle
- "Bad Vibes" – Ayra Starr
- "Bag Lady" – Erykah Badu
- "Be Alright" – Kehlani
- "Beautiful" – Christina Aguilera
- "Born Ready" – Zayde Wolf
- "Break My Soul" – Beyoncé
- "Brave" – Sara Bareilles
- "Brown Skin Girl" – Beyoncé
- "Change" – J. Cole
- "Cool People" – Chloe x Halle
- "Cranes in the Sky" – Solange
- "Die Hard" – Kendrick Lamar ft. Blxst & Amanda Reifer
- "Eye of the Tiger" – Survivor
- "Energy" – Tyla Jane
- "Fight Song" – Rachel Platten
- "Find Your Way Back" – Beyoncé
- "Free Mind" – Tems
- "Freedom" – Beyoncé ft. Kendrick Lamar
- "Glory" – Common & John Legend
- "Good Days" – Sza
- "Golden" – Jill Scott
- "Girl on Fire" – Alicia Keys

- "Healing in My Heels" – Toni Jones
- "I Gotta Find Peace of Mind" – Lauryn Hill
- "I'm Every Woman" – Whitney Houston
- "Keep Ya Head Up" – 2Pac
- "Know Your Worth" – Khalid ft. Disclosure
- "Lovely Day" – Bill Withers
- "Lift Every Voice and Sing" – Tasha Cobbs Leonard
- "Masterpiece (Mona Lisa)" – Jazmine Sullivan
- "More Than Enough" – Geminelle ft. D Smoke
- "My Power" – Beyoncé, Tierra Whack, Moonchild Sanelly & Nija
- "Not Afraid" – Eminem
- "No. 1" – Tyla ft. Tems
- "No Weapon" – Fred Hammond
- "Praying" – Kesha
- "Put It On God" – Limoblaze ft. Annatoria
- "Rise Up" – Andra Day
- "Rich Spirit" – Kendrick Lamar
- "Roar" – Katy Perry
- "Scars to Your Beautiful" – Alessia Cara
- "Shake It Out" – Florence + the Machine
- "Skyscraper" – Demi Lovato
- "Stand For Myself" – Yola
- "Stand Strong" – Davido ft. The Sunday Service Choir
- "Stand Up" – Cynthia Erivo
- "Stay with Me" – Annatoria

- "Still I Rise" – Yolanda Adams
- "Survivor" – Destiny's Child
- "The Climb" – Miley Cyrus
- "This Is Me" – Keala Settle & The Greatest Showman Ensemble
- "Three Little Birds" – Bob Marley & The Wailers
- "Titanium" – David Guetta ft. Sia
- "Turn to Gold" – Aiza
- "Unstoppable" – Sia
- "Unwritten" – Natasha Bedingfield
- "Warrior" – Demi Lovato
- "Warrior Healer" – Geminelle

About the Author

Sharisse Scott-Rawlins is a poet, fashion designer, and visionary whose work lives at the intersection of healing, creativity, and truth. A cancer survivor and Howard University MBA graduate, Sharisse transforms lived experience into art, advocacy, and safe space. Sharisse began writing these poems on the sacred sands of Inkwell Beach—her childhood sanctuary on Martha's Vineyard and a place deeply interwoven with her family's legacy. In 2016, during her battle with cancer, those shores became more than a refuge; they became her healing ground.

Dear Fellow Warrior, is her debut poetry collection— A journey of softness, survival, and self-return. Her words are both mirror and medicine —for anyone becoming who they were always meant to be. Follow **@BYSHARISSE** on all platforms or visit **bysharisse.com** to explore the living archive of *bySharisse* and get in touch!

www.ingramcontent.com/pod-product-compliance
Lightning Source LLC
Chambersburg PA
CBHW070648160426
43194CB00009B/1625